Letort Paper

REFORMING MILITARY COMMAND ARRANGEMENTS:
THE CASE OF THE RAPID DEPLOYMENT JOINT TASK FORCE

Henrik Bliddal

March 2011

*****

Comments pertaining to this report are invited and should be forwarded to: Director, Strategic Studies Institute, U.S. Army War College, 122 Forbes Ave, Carlisle, PA 17013-5244.

*****

Too many people to name have helped the author in one way or another, but he especially wishes to thank the following individuals and institutions: the Royal Danish Defence College's Institute for Strategy (under whose auspices the thesis, on which this monograph is based, was written); my interview partners; the staffs at the Jimmy Carter Library, the Library of Congress, the National Archives and Record Administration, the National Defense University and the National Security Archives; Ashwan Reddy; Frank L. Jones; Andrew Ludwig; Ingeborg Nørregaard; Ferdinand Kjærulff; Magnus Hjortdal; Mathias Lydholm Rasmussen; Bjarke Hauerslev Larsen; Jonathan Harder; Henrik Østergaard Breitenbauch; Andrea Pretis; René Rieger; Matthias Rockel; and Anders Wivel.

*****

All Strategic Studies Institute (SSI) publications may be downloaded free of charge from the SSI website. Hard copies of this report may also be obtained free of charge while supplies last by placing an order on the SSI website. The SSI website address is: *www.StrategicStudiesInstitute.army.mil*.

*****

The Strategic Studies Institute publishes a monthly e-mail newsletter to update the national security community on the research of our analysts, recent and forthcoming publications, and upcoming conferences sponsored by the Institute. Each newsletter also provides a strategic commentary by one of our research analysts. If you are interested in receiving this newsletter, please subscribe on the SSI website at *www.StrategicStudiesInstitute. army.mil/newsletter/*.

FOREWORD

Our national security system is the tool box with which we navigate an ever-changing international environment: It turns our overall capabilities into active assets, protects us against the threats of an anarchic international system and makes it possible to exploit its opportunities. Today, however, the system is arguably in dire need of reform. As Secretary of Defense Robert Gates recently argued, "The problem is not that past and present administrations have failed to recognize and clearly define national interests, but rather that the evolution of the security environment has consistently outpaced the ability of U.S. government institutions and approaches to adapt."[1]

Unfortunately, much remains in the dark about how the organizations that safeguard our national security are reformed as international circumstances change. In this monograph, Mr. Henrik Bliddal sheds some light on this question by examining a crucial historical case of military reform: the establishment of the Rapid Deployment Joint Task Force (RDJTF)—the direct predecessor of the United States Central Command (CENTCOM).

The monograph demonstrates how the U.S. military adapted to the emerging security challenges in the Persian Gulf in the late 1970s by recasting military command arrangements. The RDJTF—although only an interim solution on the way to Central Command—was one of the components of President Jimmy Carter's Persian Gulf Security Framework, which marked a critical strategic reorientation towards the region as a vital battleground in the global competition with the Soviet Union. Based upon original interviews with key civilians and military officers as well as extensive archival research—including the analysis of material only recently declassified—this monograph is the most complete account of the establishment of the RDJTF thus far.

Going beyond mere history, Mr. Bliddal also suggests how national security reforms can be understood more generally. In this way, he lays out some of the challenges that we face today with effectively restructuring our security and defense establishment. Especially in these times of fiscal restraint, a better grasp of institutional reform is very much needed. The Strategic Studies Institute is pleased to present this thorough study of a historic case that can teach us lessons pertaining to our problems today.

DOUGLAS C. LOVELACE, JR.
Director
Strategic Studies Institute

ENDNOTE - FOREWORD

1. Robert Gates as quoted in "Gates Disputes Blue-Ribbon Panel's Criticism of QDR Report," *Inside the Navy*, August 8, 2010, available from *InsideDefense.com*.

ABOUT THE AUTHOR

HENRIK BLIDDAL is the Director of the Science and Technology Committee at the North Atlantic Treaty Organization (NATO) Parliamentary Assembly in Brussels, Belgium. He is also co-editor with Peter Wilson and Casper Sylvest of the book, *Classics of International Relations* (forthcoming 2012). Mr. Bliddal has earlier worked as the editor of the Danish peer-reviewed, social science journal, *Politik*, and has written a case study on the U.S. intervention in Liberia in 2003 for the Project on National Security Reform (PNSR), which will be published as part of a collection of case studies in a volume edited jointly by the PNSR and the Strategic Studies Institute (forthcoming 2010/11). Mr. Bliddal holds an M.Sc. in political science from the University of Copenhagen, Denmark.

SUMMARY

After the Shah of Iran was deposed and the Soviet Union invaded Afghanistan in 1979, the United States began to craft a new Persian Gulf Security Framework (PGSF). Consisting of military, diplomatic, economic, and covert steps, it signified a historic strategic reorientation towards the Persian Gulf. This paper examines an integral part of the PGSF: the creation of the Rapid Deployment Joint Task Force (RDJTF). As the first real tool for U.S. power projection in the area, and the immediate precursor to today's Central Command (CENTCOM), the RDJTF has indeed left an important mark on the U.S. approach to the Persian Gulf. This paper is the fullest account of its creation thus far.

The RDJTF is both an example of forward strategic thinking as well as one of organizational resistance and competing understandings of the international environment. In Jimmy Carter's first year as President, the administration recognized an acute weakness in U.S. power projection capabilities and consequently mandated the creation of a Rapid Deployment Force (RDF). However, for almost 2 years, nothing happened because the U.S. military services were not interested in such an RDF. Differences at the senior level about how to react to Soviet actions in the Persian Gulf provided additional cover for the military to ignore the RDF. Only the fall of the Iranian regime in early 1979 put the RDF back on the agenda. However, the military was soon locked into an interservice quarrel that pitted the Army against the Marine Corps. A compromise was adopted in October 1979 that established a semi-autonomous RDJTF to be led by a Marine commander under an Army superior and with a global role, but an initial focus on the Persian Gulf. At the same time, key figures on the National Security Council staff started advocating for a separate unified command for Southwest Asia. After the Soviet invasion of Afghanistan, they were able to push harder for this objective, but gridlock in the military services was now joined by a struggle for control between the Marine commander of the RDJTF and his Army superior. Even though the costs of delayed RDF implementation became clear, when a serious Soviet military threat to Iran emerged in the summer of 1980, the Carter administration was still not able to establish a unified command, which had to wait until President Ronald Reagan's terms in office.

Today, policy advocates are calling for wide-ranging changes in the way the United States is organized to meet the threats of a new security environment. In this light, the case of the RDJTF takes on additional significance, since it represents a major adjustment in a changing international environment. For despite all the advocacy and activity, still too little is known about the difficulties that so often plague reform processes. This paper therefore turns to the past to recognize some of the challenges ahead. Thus, even though the national security system has changed greatly over the past 30 years, this paper ends with the suggestion that the underlying mechanics of reform have not changed and lays out a model for understanding national security reforms. It is argued that efforts at national security system reform are caught between two logics: Policymakers push to adapt to shifting international conditions, but national security organizations continually strive for greater autonomy in the national security system and bigger shares of the budget. These two logics are most often at odds, thus producing sub-optimal results. Further studies of the reform processes are therefore essential. It is not enough to know how best to rearrange the system, which is a very difficult task in itself. Equally important, the organizational hurdles for reform must be analyzed much more closely. Only then will the United States be able to take real steps to improve its institutional capacity to deal with the challenges of the 21st century.

REFORMING MILITARY COMMAND ARRANGEMENTS: THE CASE OF THE RAPID DEPLOYMENT JOINT TASK FORCE

LONG-TERM STRATEGIC THINKING MEETS ORGANIZATIONAL POLITICS[1]

> In the Middle East, [the Soviets] are in possibly the weakest position since they entered the area in 1956.[2]
>
> — National Security Advisor Zbigniew Brzezinski, February 26, 1977

> Let our position be absolutely clear: An attempt by any outside force to gain control of the Persian Gulf region will be regarded as an assault on the vital interests of the United States of America, and such an assault will be repelled by any means necessary, including military force.[3] [The Carter Doctrine]
>
> — President Jimmy Carter, January 23, 1980

It is a long way between Zbigniew Brzezinski's assessment of the Soviet position in the Middle East and the Carter Doctrine formulated by President Carter a month after the Soviet invasion of Afghanistan. Over the course of Carter's presidency (1977-81), fundamental changes occurred on the international stage. After Richard Nixon had moved the relationship between the United States and the Soviet Union towards détente, the Carter administration was faced with an ever more assertive Soviet regime. The changing tide was nowhere more evident than in the "arc of crisis"[4] that stretched from the Horn of Africa through the

Arabian Peninsula to Pakistan. By 1979, the U.S. security framework for this region was indeed in ruins, as the fall of the Shah in Iran and the Soviet invasion of Afghanistan had destroyed the local equilibrium, and the world soon witnessed renewed and intense competition between the two superpowers.

The steps taken after Ayatollah Khomeini seized power in Tehran and the Soviets marched into Kabul have been described as an "important and far-reaching redirection of U.S. geopolitical strategy."[5] To rebuild the U.S. position in the region, the Carter administration introduced a new Persian Gulf Security Framework (PGSF), consisting of a number of military, diplomatic, economic, and covert steps.

This paper examines an integral part of the PGSF: the creation of the Rapid Deployment Joint Task Force (RDJTF), the immediate precursor to today's United States Central Command (CENTCOM). It examines the origins of the RDJTF in much greater detail than previous studies[6] and contrasts the generally negative, but often superficial, view of President Carter's national security politics with the realities in the administration (which, granted, were frequently ill-communicated to the U.S. public).[7]

The importance of the PGSF and the RDJTF, as pieces of Cold War history, should not be underestimated. The late General William E. Odom, Brzezinski's military assistant under Carter and later Director of the National Security Agency, has argued in an article on the RDJTF that the development of the PGSF "was critical to the success of Operations DESERT SHIELD and DESERT STORM in 1990-1991, the toppling of the Taliban and Al Qaeda in Afghanistan in 2001-2002, the U.S. invasion of Iraq in 2003, and many smaller operations in the 1980s and 1990s."[8] The Carter years thus introduced a "switch in U.S. priorities, away from the Northeast Asian and European theatre[s] and in favour of the Persian Gulf region"[9]—a switch that is arguably still ongoing. In his article, Odom concedes that he was not able to tell the full story of the RDJTF, but he hoped to "inspire some scholar to undertake a full account in the future."[10] Historical examination is never complete, but this paper aspires to be the fullest account yet, resting on original research in U.S. archives and interviews with participants in the policy processes at the time.[11]

However, more than just a history of the origins of CENTCOM and the beginning of a deeper strategic involvement with the Persian Gulf region,[12] the story of the RDJTF as an example of organizational reform in the U.S. military tells an all-too-familiar tale: long-term strategic thinking meeting parochial service interests in the pre-Goldwater-Nichols era.[13] It is in this light that the case of the RDJTF takes on added significance today. In the wake of the terrorist attacks of September 11, 2001 (9/11), vocal calls for changes in the national security apparatus have once again emerged, arguing that the U.S. national security system is in dire need of adapting to a changing threat environment. Some reforms have taken place, but it is clear that there is still a long way to go in reforming the U.S. national security establishment.

The final report of the 9/11 Commission concluded that the failures in the lead-up to the attacks were "symptoms of the government's broader inability to adapt how it manages problems to the new challenges of the twenty-first century."[14] In a recent large-scale review of the U.S. national security system, the conclusions were similar: The Guiding Coalition of the Project on National Security Reform (PNSR), which included such luminaries as General James L. Jones, Joseph S. Nye, Jr., and Brent Scowcroft, warned that "the national security system of the United States is increasingly misaligned with a rapidly changing global security environment."[15] They go on to suggest that "the United States simply cannot afford the failure rate that the current national security system is not only prone but virtually guaranteed to cause" and that, in the absence of further reforms, "even the wisest men and women upon whom we come to depend are doomed to see their most solid policy understandings crumble into the dust of failure."[16]

Interestingly, despite all the advocacy and policy activity, still far too little is known about the obstacles that have plagued reforms over the years.[17] If the United States is to successfully rearrange its national security organizations, the underlying mechanics of reforms have to be more fully understood. One way to better understand the processes of reform is to turn to the past to recognize the challenges ahead. This paper therefore ends with a suggestion on how reform processes can be understood more generally. It argues that, while the context of reforms will change, the core logic of reform does not. It is thus hoped that this paper can shed some light on national security reform processes to point to better solutions in the future. For even the best policy advice will fail if one does not know how to favorably shape the process and implement the reform decisions.

THE STONY ROAD TOWARDS THE RDJTF

The analysis of the RDJTF falls into five parts. First, the context of the incoming Carter administration is provided by briefly reviewing U.S. strategy in the Persian Gulf between World War II and 1977. Second, the period from the inauguration of President Carter until the fall of the Shah of Iran is examined. Third, the time between the Iranian Revolution and the Soviet invasion of Afghanistan is analyzed. Fourth, the crucial period between the invasion and President Reagan's inauguration, including an account of the Soviet military threat to Iran and the Persian Gulf as a whole, is scrutinized. Fifth, an epilogue is offered that briefly explains the way to the creation of CENTCOM.

THE LEGACY: U.S. STRATEGY IN THE PERSIAN GULF BEFORE 1977

Before analyzing the Carter administration's engagement with the Persian Gulf, it is helpful to understand the policies and military command arrangements that the new administration inherited. The Nixon and Gerald Ford years had bestowed upon President Carter a low-profile military strategy towards the Persian Gulf. In fact, the Middle East had never commanded the same attention as Europe and Northeast Asia in U.S. grand strategy before Carter's election: The United States had no formal treaty relationships in the Middle East, and little in-depth military planning and presence existed.[18]

Traditionally, the United Kingdom (UK) had provided a security umbrella for the Middle East. However, after World War II and especially after the Suez Crisis of 1956, it increasingly withdrew from the region. U.S. strategic interaction with the area has thus been described as compensating for the waning British presence. In 1957, in reaction to fears that the Union of Soviet Socialist Republics (USSR) would intervene on Egypt's behalf in the Suez Canal Crisis, the Eisenhower Doctrine was formulated, which promised economic and military assistance for states in the region against Soviet intrusions.[19] President Eisenhower also focused on the stability of the so-called Northern Tier states (Turkey, Iraq, Iran, and Pakistan) by supporting the UK-led Baghdad Pact (later renamed the Central Treaty Organization after Iraq dropped out) and by signing security agreements with Turkey, Iran, and Pakistan in 1959.

In 1971, the UK practically disengaged from the region when it withdrew its military forces from all its bases that were "east-of-Suez," most importantly from Yemen, the states on the Persian Gulf, Malaysia, and Singapore. Unsurprisingly, the USSR tried to fill the ensuing power vacuum by, for example, signing a friendship treaty with Iraq in 1972.[20] President Nixon responded by drawing on his own 3-year-old Nixon Doctrine, which emphasized that U.S. allies had to rely on self-defense first, if they wanted to be covered by the U.S. security umbrella.[21] Thus, the United States conceived of the so-called Twin Pillar strategy, which centered on Iran and Saudi Arabia as its primary allies in the Gulf. This reflected, in the words of the State Department, "the assumption that regional dynamics were, in large measure, adequate to deal with local problems."[22]

In terms of military command arrangements, the Joint Chiefs of Staff (JCS) decided to create a Middle East Command in 1956, but the State Department objected, and nothing ever came of it.[23] Thus, shifting arrangements for the Middle East prevailed until 1963, when the Congo civil war prompted the United States to assign the Middle East, Sub-Saharan Africa, and Southern Asia to the newly-created Strike Command (STRICOM), which was charged with reinforcing other commands and carrying out certain contingency operations. Under Nixon, however, budget cuts and increasing aversion to Vietnam-like interventions led to divestment of STRICOM's area responsibilities and a name change to Readiness Command (REDCOM). By 1977, responsibility for the Persian Gulf region was therefore split between European Command (EUCOM) on land and Pacific Command (PACOM) on sea.

In sum, President Carter inherited a strategy towards the Persian Gulf that relied on the capabilities of regional allies to preserve U.S. interests and a military command arrangement that split the region between EUCOM and PACOM.

FROM CARTER'S INAUGURATION TO THE FALL OF THE SHAH

Détente and the Persian Gulf in 1977.

From the outset, the Carter administration followed a strategy that would reestablish U.S.-Soviet détente and stabilize the military equilibrium between the two superpowers. Carter also introduced a number of new, "idealist" foreign policy goals, such as restraint on arms sales in order to reduce military competition. In the Persian Gulf region, it was thought that the Twin Pillars strategy and the countries it primarily rested on, Iran and Saudi Arabia, were stable, and that political trends were adverse to Soviet interests.

President Carter had entered office at a difficult juncture in U.S. history. As the country struggled in the aftermath of the Vietnam War and the Watergate scandal, the President was confronted with a multitude of difficult issues. After a year in office, the National Security Council (NSC) staff looked back upon the rather poor inheritance they felt President Ford had left them in 1977:

> Our allies were uneasy about our constancy, our will and our ability to lead. Our adversaries were openly speculating about the political consequences of "the general crisis of capitalism." The Third World was generally hostile or disappointed. The American public distrusted our policies and deplored the apparent lack of moral content in our actions and goals.[24]

The President and his advisors believed that they were faced with a similar situation as that which faced President Harry S. Truman in the wake of World War II. A redirection of U.S. foreign policy was necessary, and nothing less than a new international system, increasingly involving all states, was the ultimate goal. Carter distinctively broadened U.S. foreign policy goals in opposition to the Nixon/Henry Kissinger approach. Ten policy objectives topped Carter's foreign policy list, when he entered office:

1. Stronger ties with Western Europe, Japan and other advanced democracies.

2. Development of a worldwide net of bilateral cooperation with emerging regional powers.

3. Improved North-South relations.

4. Development of a more comprehensive and reciprocal détente with the USSR.

5. Normalization of the U.S.-Chinese relationship.

6. A comprehensive Middle Eastern settlement.

7. Progressive change in Africa.

8. Disarmament and nuclear nonproliferation.

9. Increasing focus on human rights.

10. Restoration of strong U.S. and North Atlantic Treaty Organization (NATO) defense postures.

Indicative of reorienting U.S. foreign policy towards issues other than the U.S.-USSR relationship was the fact that the USSR was not even mentioned in his inaugural speech.[25] This, of course, did not mean that the USSR was not still of central concern. On the contrary, the U.S.-Soviet relationship would soon and quite forcefully come back on the agenda.

At the beginning, Carter's National Security Advisor, Zbigniew Brzezinski, was hopeful that a meaningful détente with the USSR could be reestablished after it had been strained in recent years. A month after the inauguration, he argued that "Brezhnev has made a personal and public commitment to reestablishing the 'detente' policy."[26] After the election, the USSR, in his view, wanted to show "that detente could be set back but not fundamentally altered."[27]

Already in the summer of 1977, Brzezinski saw some clouds on the horizon, however, especially regarding the Strategic Arms Limitations Talks.[28] Nevertheless, William Hyland, an NSC staffer on the USSR and East Europe desk, argued in a June 1977 memorandum forwarded to Carter that "too much of the current analysis focuses on the transitory, while disregarding the permanent problems confronting the USSR." He came to the conclusion that "many of the permanent factors seem to point to an eventual turn in Soviet policy back toward something resembling 'détente'."[29] A couple of weeks later, however, Brzezinski wrote the President that "your first period of true testing in international affairs is now upon us" — not least in the U.S.-USSR relationship.[30] When 1977 drew to a close, the State Department ended on a rather upbeat note, however, writing that "the Soviets have on a whole been rather forthcoming," while still noting "potentially disruptive developments."[31]

The United States was also optimistic regarding the Persian Gulf. Historically, Russia had had an interest in obtaining access to the Persian Gulf, but there was "little direct evidence" that the USSR was "actively pursuing that goal."[32] In fact, the USSR had not been able to capitalize on the British withdrawal from "east-of-Suez," as its treaty with Iraq had been the only significant gain, and relations with most states had worsened (even with Iraq).[33] More importantly, it had suffered a severe loss with the expulsion from Egypt in 1972. In December 1976, the Central Intelligence Agency (CIA) had thus assessed that trends were clearly detrimental to Soviet interests in the Gulf/Peninsula region. Nevertheless, the USSR could bide its time, since opportunities could quickly present themselves. Furthermore, because of its energy independence, it possessed no vital interests in the region. Consequently, in the eyes of the CIA, the USSR had the (mostly negative) goal of depriving the West of influence, leading to an expectation of a lower level of effort and less inclination to risk confrontation with the United States.

Carter's promise of a more moral and humane foreign policy also played a role regarding the Persian Gulf. One goal was "to limit the world's armaments to those necessary for each nation's own domestic safety."[34] A policy of unilateral restraint on arms transfers was therefore soon joined with U.S.-Soviet negotiations under the banner of the Conventional Arms Transfer and Indian Ocean talks.[35] Whereas the former sought to reduce global arms transfers, the latter were meant to stabilize U.S.-Soviet regional competition. After all, the military balance in the region seemed to favor the United States.[36] The USSR, after some hesitation, made an initial commitment to these two initiatives, but states in the Persian Gulf increasingly began to doubt U.S. commitment to the region as a consequence.[37]

An Early Strategy Review and the Need for Rapid Deployment Forces.

As in most administrations, Carter initiated a thorough review of U.S. national strategy early on.[38] On February 18, 1977, he signed Presidential Review Memorandum (PRM) 10, which directed that "a comprehensive examination be made of overall U.S. national strategy and capabilities."[39] PRM-10 had two components: a Military Force Posture Review and a Comprehensive Net Assessment.[40] While the former dealt with global military strategies, the latter was a dynamic review and looked at "past, present, and probable future trends in the evolution of the principal capabilities" between the eastern and western bloc.[41]

The Comprehensive Net Assessment concluded that a rough overall equivalence existed in conventional military capabilities and an essential equivalence in nuclear forces.[42] Crucially, however, while the United States was significantly ahead and likely to remain so in all nonmilitary aspects of power, future trends in every military category were adverse.[43] In regional terms, the outlook was difficult in Europe; equilibrium had developed in Northeast Asia; and the Persian Gulf "had become vital to the West and also vulnerable to the combination of internal fragility and growing Soviet power projection into the region."[44] The Gulf was still not on par with Europe and Northeast Asia in importance, but it was clear to the Carter administration that it had become much more central to global geopolitics.

Soviet power projection capabilities had become of critical concern, according to the Comprehensive Net Assessment. In this respect, the Persian Gulf was especially worrisome because the two superpowers had "about equal ability to project forces" into the region.[45] Since the Comprehensive Net Assessment also judged that "the Soviets would now be more prone to use military power for political ends," the need for increased capabilities to respond to global contingencies was clear. It was thus agreed that forces for crisis management and local wars should be added on top of those required for a NATO-Warsaw Pact war.[46] The most relevant areas for such a highly responsive, global strike force were the Middle East, the Persian Gulf and Korea.

Rapid deployment was particularly important in the Gulf because Iran had been identified as the most likely locale for a Soviet-induced crisis confrontation. Summarizing the relevant study paper, Brzezinski told Carter:

> The paper identifies Iran as the "one contiguous non-satellite state" that could be the "possible site for a Soviet-initiated [crisis confrontation]." It meets the criteria which Soviet leaders and planners might use if they were consciously attempting to expand their influence through the political use of military force and wished to confront the U.S. with a situation in which it would suffer a diplomatic humiliation if it made no response or would risk military defeat if it made a military response.[47]

A requirement for the development of a rapid deployment force (RDF) was thus written into Presidential Directive (PD) 18 ("U.S. National Strategy") that resulted from the PRM-10 process: "[T]he United

States will maintain a deployment force of light divisions with strategic mobility independent of overseas bases and logistical support, which includes moderate naval and tactical air forces, and limited land combat forces."[48]

It should be noted here that the RDF requirement should not be seen as the beginning of a new overall strategy in the Gulf. It is better understood as a planned military tool that was supposed to bolster regional strategies, such as the Twin Pillar strategy. Indeed, after PRM-10/PD-18 had been issued, it was the negative trends in Europe that commanded the administration's attention for the most part. Furthermore, in Odom's view, the RDF largely slipped into PD-18 because no one seriously cared about it other than a number of NSC staffers (in particular Odom himself and Samuel Huntington, who was an NSC staffer on national security planning at the time):

> Although only a few agency participants supported the RDF proposal, others did not seriously object to including it in PD-18. Locked into their daily routines and worried mainly about current problems, the skeptics probably viewed it as largely academic and not worth a quarrel.[49]

The PD-18 process also revealed the first differences of opinion in the administration about its strategy towards the Persian Gulf. Most policymakers wanted to deal with the Persian Gulf via détente and arms control efforts, but some, particularly on the NSC staff, were very concerned with the Soviet military buildup and the region's criticality to the United States.[50] At the time of PD-18, the former side prevailed, and most of the strategic attention was devoted to détente, Europe, the Egyptian-Israeli peace process, and China.[51] William Quandt, an NSC staffer for the Middle East and North Africa at the time, did not sense "that there was any strong sentiment that [the United States] needed a significant upgrading of military capabilities in the Gulf."[52]

Soviet Actions from the Horn of Africa to Afghanistan.

The first 2 years of the Carter presidency were busy ones: rebuilding détente, reinvigorating NATO, moving towards closer ties with China, resolution of the Panama Canal issue, crafting an Egyptian-Israeli peace, reformulation of nuclear strategy, and the infusion of human rights concerns into global politics. It is thus not surprising that the United States relied on its friends, Iran and Saudi Arabia, to safeguard its interests in the Persian Gulf region. Soon, however, Soviet actions made it unavoidable to take a closer look at regional security.

It was a conflict in the Horn of Africa that revealed profound differences within the administration on its regional security policy. Traditionally a U.S. client, a revolutionary government in Ethiopia had recently moved closer to the USSR. When it decided to expel most U.S. personnel, the Soviet Union found itself in the position of being the patron of both Ethiopia and Somalia, with which it had long entertained close ties. In the summer of 1977, however, Siad Barré, Somalia's heavy-handed dictator, decided to invade Ethiopia's Ogaden region, which Somalia had claimed for a long time. After Soviet-led negotiations failed to produce a settlement, the USSR dropped Somalia as a client and instead undertook a massive military airlift in support of Ethiopia (and Cuban forces). Somalia consequently sought closer contacts with the United States. As an Ethiopian intrusion loomed large, the United States thus faced a severe dilemma: Could it afford to acquiesce in the Soviet show of force, be left without any allies in the Horn, and lose standing with Somalia's Arab and Iranian backers, or should the United States support an aggressor and violate its new policies on arms sales and human rights?

The issue came to a head in a meeting on February 22, 1978, where it was discussed whether to send an aircraft carrier to deter an Ethiopian intrusion. Brzezinski advocated it; Secretary of State Cyrus Vance emphatically opposed it; and, ultimately, Secretary of Defense Harold Brown could not see much value in it, either. Brzezinski argued that a carrier would be "a confidence building measure" to assure the local states of U.S. presence and will, as well as its determination to protect arms flows and to provide protection against the USSR.[53] He feared the consequences of an Ethiopian invasion because it "would contribute to uncertainty and destabilization in Egypt, Saudi Arabia, and Iran." States would feel "that if they are in a contest, they should not get caught relying on the United States." Vance strongly disagreed and "hated to see Somalia characterized as a friend we are letting down." He instead argued that the United States should keep its forces out, even if Ethiopia crossed the border, and seek a political solution (possibly followed by arms sales). Otherwise, the United States would be playing a bluff that it could not carry through. Brown shared Brzezinski's concerns and argued that the United States could not "let the Soviets fish in troubled waters." However, he was skeptical of the military merits of sending a carrier, even though he was inclined to support it, if the Iranians or Saudi sent troops to Somalia. In the end, he did not take Brzezinski's side, since he saw failure as too likely, which would have had serious repercussions, as it would have reduced the credibility of U.S. task forces in the future. After the meeting, the President did not support the move either.[54]

This episode would prove important since it demonstrated the very different views on Soviet behavior in the Third World and the strategic importance of assuring allies in the Persian Gulf. Brzezinski attributed this split over policy to different views of détente in the administration. One view, close to his own, asserted that the Soviets had "stomped all over the code of détente."[55] Others argued that recent Soviet actions had to be considered case by case, and they were, in general, "acting on traditional lines and essentially reacting to U.S. steps."

Brzezinski, however, continued to contend that the USSR had violated the jointly agreed rules of détente with their actions in Ethiopia, Yemen, and Afghanistan. After a coup in South Yemen, he pointed to the vulnerability of U.S. allies in the Gulf, as he saw the balance in the region shifting:

> [T]he Soviets, having installed their crew in Kabul [The USSR had already supported a coup in Afghanistan earlier that year], having attempted the same in Baghdad, with Addis in their pocket, have now added another link in the ever-tighter chain encircling the moderate Arabs.

Some tentative discussions on regional security occurred during the remainder of 1978, but they remained rather vague and without much direction.[56] Most, especially in the State Department, remained unconvinced that a comprehensive security framework could be created for the region. For example, a State

Department paper questioned whether the region was amenable "to support a unique regional concept and the consequent application of a consistent single U.S. strategy" and whether regional states would "support a dramatic U.S. military or political response."[57] In an argument that the Department would later take up again, it saw a danger that U.S. actions in the region could indeed be counterproductive, driving Arab states away from, rather than toward, the U.S. security umbrella.

The fact that the Iranian regime was not yet seen at grave risk of collapse very likely contributed to a missing focus on the region. For example, on November 3, 1978, Brzezinski still told the President: "Good news! According to a CIA assessment, issued in August, Iran is not in a revolutionary or even a 'pre-revolutionary' situation."[58] More remarkably, only 2 months before the Shah left Iran, the U.S. ambassador for the first time raised the possibility of his downfall.[59]

At the policymaking level, Brzezinski and some NSC staffers stood alone in their dour view of the region. In a tragic case of foresight, Brzezinski probably wrote his most famous memo on December 2, 1978.[60] He warned of an emerging "arc of crisis"—stretching "from Chittagona (Bangladesh) through Islamabad to Aden"—where the United States was most vulnerable. He indeed saw "the beginning of a major crisis." Since friendly states in the region felt that the United States would not or could not "offer effective political and military protection," Soviet-friendly groups were free to exploit the political vacuum. This led him to the following conclusion:

[T]he West as a whole may be faced with a challenge of historic proportions. A shift in Iranian/Saudi orientation would have a direct impact on [U.S.-European-

Japanese] cohesion, and it would induce in time more "neutralist" attitudes on the part of some of our key allies. In a sentence, it would mean a fundamental shift in the global structure of power.

The events in 1977/1978 showed that the administration was split on whether the regional military balance in the Persian Gulf was shifting at all, whether it was worth risking the global strategy of détente, and whether increased military presence would assure or alienate friends. The events in Iran would soon force the United States to define its regional balancing strategy much more clearly than it had in the past, but the policy differences would only partially disappear. Before the consequences of the Iranian Revolution can be addressed, the organizational response to the PD-18 requirement to establish an RDF must be considered, however.

Organizational Disinterest in the Rapid Deployment Force.

In 1977-78, implementing the RDF requirement of PD-18 was arguably at the bottom of the agenda in the Department of Defense (DoD) and the military. No organization saw any benefits to be gained by taking up the issue: There was virtually no money allotted for the task; other requirements weighed heavily on the military; a latent resistance to look at command arrangements existed; and no real pressure from the political level was forthcoming.

Indeed, in the declassified material that was available for this paper, there is but one brief mention of the implementation of the RDF in connection with a JCS Limited Contingency Study for a Petroleum Supply Vulnerability Assessment. However, even this study looked only at what type of capabilities were needed for contingencies in the Persian Gulf region.[61] This arguably seems far from an actual implementation effort. Yet, the absence of discussion on the RDF requirement speaks volumes, as there were no real incentives to tackle it.

First, no real funding was set aside for an RDF. As a reason for the lack of efforts to establish the RDF, a DoD paper would later argue that "most of the programmatic decisions" for the budget for Fiscal Year 1979 (October 1, 1978-September 30, 1979) had already been made before PD-18 was signed.[62] Without funding, Odom argues, DoD "lacked the resources to create [an RDF], having experienced a 38 percent decline in its budget since 1968."[63]

Second, the highest defense priorities in the wake of PD-18 were nuclear modernization programs and NATO reinvigoration. Taking up the RDF challenge would have created an additional burden on the DoD and the Services. As Njølstad argues, "it went without saying that it would be difficult, if not impossible, to maintain a credible forward defence posture in Europe and build a rapid deployment capability in other regions at the same time."[64] Robert Murray, who was Deputy Assistant Secretary of Defense for International Security Affairs and later Undersecretary of the Navy under President Carter, points in the same direction:

> A lot of our attention and devotion . . . —in the budget—was to that shifting of the strategy from a 'nuclear-first' to a 'conventional-first' strategy [in Europe], which required a lot of effort on the part of the European Command [which was also in charge of the Persian Gulf countries] and so forth.[65]

Third, as the RDF was supposed to be a joint venture between the military Services, it is highly likely that none of them cared much about implementing it. In fact, there is no reason to believe that the intense organizational struggles between the Services that would take place, when the administration pushed for implementation later would not have taken place in 1977 or 1978 as well.

Fourth, there was—in Odom's words—"no real sponsor outside the NSC for an increased security effort for the Persian Gulf,"[66] i.e., there was no pressure from the senior policy level. Along these lines, Brown suggests "that part of the reason that there was not a rapid implementation of PD-18 was that the specific contingencies seemed remote."[67] Indeed, Odom would later tell Brzezinski:

> Convinced that they would demilitarize the Indian Ocean, the [International Security Affairs] staff in Defense had no time or enthusiasm for the RDF. They got lots of encouragement from State and no discouragement from NSC regional and security clusters.[68]

The State Department, as Odom argues, "tended to view any larger U.S. military presence as provocative to radical political groups throughout the Arab world" and was thus not very interested in the RDF.[69] With a lot to lose and nothing to gain for the DoD, the State Department, and the military Services, it is not surprising that no one took up the RDF challenge before the Iranian Revolution compelled the administration to again think about basic U.S. strategy in the Persian Gulf and to push for a change. Even though negative trends regarding power projection capabilities led to the requirement to establish an RDF, in the absence of consensus at the top, and with a political focus on other foreign and security priorities, such as normalizing the U.S.-China relationship, the road to the Camp David Accords, or the reinvigoration of NATO, the RDF could be safely ignored by the DoD and the military, which saw no incentives to tackle it.

FROM THE FALL OF THE SHAH TO THE INVASION OF AFGHANISTAN

First Steps towards a New Regional Security Framework.

When the Shah of Iran had to go into exile, an important U.S. ally was removed from the regional equation in the Gulf. This spawned renewed strategic thinking. The DoD began to slowly come around to NSC staff preferences, which started isolating the State Department. Brzezinski was the first to press for an increased regional commitment, development of a regional geopolitical dialogue and enhanced military presence.[70] In February 1979, Brown was sent on the first trip by a U.S. Secretary of Defense to Egypt, Saudi Arabia, and Jordan. He "did assure them — and had the agreement of the President to be able to assure them — that we were prepared to defend them."[71] Soon, according to Odom, the Conventional Arms Transfer and Indian Ocean talks "were no longer in the foreground," and the improvement of military presence "had become a legitimate step."[72]

On February 28, 1979, the NSC staffer Fritz Ermarth was arguably the first to put the new situation into an overall strategic picture with his paper, "Consultative Security Framework for the Middle East,"[73] which would serve as a reference point for Brzezinski in the coming months. He argued that the future of regional states, especially of U.S. allies, had become "uncertain and threatening." They lacked "confidence in the direction of U.S. policy and in the willingness of the United States to use its power in behalf of their security." He therefore recommended the creation of a new security framework that would neither be "a formal alliance system" nor "simply another name for bilateral cooperation on security issues." Instead regional allies should realize common interests and cooperate on security issues. Crucially, he also called for an "East-of-Suez Command entity of some kind, located in the United States but equipped to move."

The differing approaches towards U.S. strategy vis-à-vis the USSR were revealed again, however, when Brzezinski sent out Comprehensive Net Assessment 1978, a follow-up to PRM-10, on March 30, 1979.[74] It maintained that the overall conclusions of PRM-10 were still valid, but noted Soviet gains in the Persian Gulf, Middle East and Africa, an improving European balance, and a continuing negative trend in Soviet power projection capabilities. While Brown reacted positively, the State Department took issue with the study, arguing that the "appraisals of strategic and power projection trends are too somber [and] the positive NATO trends may be somewhat overstated."[75]

A turning point came at a meeting on May 11.[76] All participants agreed that the Saudis had "lost confidence in the United States' ability to help them manage their security problems." In order to reverse that perception, a number of military options were to be studied, including an enhancement of naval presence, pre-positioning of military equipment in the area, and increases in rapid deployment capabilities.

After the meeting, the DoD increasingly engaged in broader strategic thinking.[77] The next critical steps came at two meetings on June 21 and 22. Before the meetings, Ermarth judged that they "could be among the most significant of this Administration."[78] He felt that the United States was "now getting down to hard military business."

The State Department, the Central Intelligence Agency (CIA), and DoD all prepared papers on U.S. regional strategy for these meetings. Only the DoD paper and a preparatory JCS study have thus far been declassified, but the direction of the other papers can be derived from NSC staff comments. In the eyes of two NSC staffers critical of the paper, the State Department contribution was inconclusive; it provided "little basis for decision," failed to address fundamental questions, and was "aimed at discounting the need for increases in U.S. permanent military presence."[79] Instead, it argued that the Egyptian-Israeli peace process needed to "continue to have the highest priority in U.S. regional policy." Even though the State Department and CIA seemed to be open to some increase in U.S. presence, the staffers noted that the papers "clearly go to great lengths . . . to stress the penalties of adverse local reaction and the case for great moderation." Here, as in the episode in the Ethiopian-Somali war, the State Department called attention to the possibility that increasing U.S. capabilities might indeed be detrimental to U.S. policies: Regional states, feeling the pressure of internal opposition, could distance themselves from the United States, thus undermining the value of increased U.S. presence.

In contrast, the JCS and DoD papers clearly pointed towards the need for more military presence. On the whole, the JCS recommended enhanced involvement, greater assertiveness, and a coherent regional strategy, while still emphasizing the need for local states to "bear the burden of their own security."[80] They argued that "the trends in both the strategic nuclear and conventional measures of military power have encouraged the Soviet leaders to continue their probes and to press more forcefully in areas beyond the relatively secure barriers in Europe and Asia." The development of a comprehensive strategy was seen as a long-term process, but short-term steps had to be taken as well — even at the risk of degrading U.S. defense posture in Europe or the Pacific, showing how serious the JCS took the shifts in the balance. A direct intervention in Iran by the Soviets was already seen as a grave danger, but was "unlikely short of a world war scenario." It was improbable that NATO allies would redirect resources to the Gulf, they argued. Thus, the United States had to "develop the capability to project a multidivisional force from [the continental United States], supported by air and naval forces" — in other words, an RDF. An indicator of the unwillingness to look at the accompanying command arrangements of such a force is the fact that the suggestion to "[a]nalyze the present U.S. command and control structure for the area to see if modification is required" was buried deep in the paper.

The DoD paper continued along the same lines. It defined U.S. goals in the region as (a) continued U.S. and allied access to oil, (b) the security of Israel and (c) minimization of Soviet influence.[81] The fundamental questions were thus to what degree support for self-defense and/or U.S. military presence and capability in the region had to be increased. Crucially, in light of later realities, the paper assessed that regional crises would have long lead times and that the USSR would not move through Iran if it wanted to meddle in the Gulf. This led to the judgment that "the United States could surge more capable ground, naval, and tactical air forces than the Soviets to the Persian Gulf in the first thirty days of a conflict" — an assumption that had to be substantially revised barely a year later.

In the actual meeting, according to Odom, the State Department "made as strong an argument as possible against the increased military presence" and "went so far as to argue that an increased U.S. presence would look to Moscow as a new and different balance."[82] Nevertheless, Brzezinski and Brown were on the same page at the meeting, and Brzezinski was able to bring the President aboard afterwards. It was therefore decided to increase the naval U.S. Middle East Force (MIDEASTFOR) in Bahrain from three to five or six combat vessels and to deploy four combatant elements to the region annually. These meetings thus marked the point, when the majority of senior policymakers had switched from reluctance to a willingness to strengthen military capabilities in the region, with the State Department increasingly relegated to the sidelines.

From the Concept of a Rapid Deployment Force to the Rapid Deployment Joint Task Force.

On June 22, 1979, Brown ordered the JCS to revise the command plan to implement the RDF requirement, marking the beginning of an intense interservice quarrel, which primarily pitted the Army against the Marine Corps. The JCS and the Services were not thrilled: Assigning and redistributing command responsibilities can always disturb the delicate balance of generals between the Services, especially in the days prior to the Goldwater-Nichols Act. Christopher Shoemaker, who was a staffer at the Office for International Security Affairs and from October 1979 Assistant to Odom on the NSC staff, argues that: "There are few documents more sacred than the UCP [the Unified Command Plan]. It involves four-star billets and therefore it is very, very contentious in the Joint Chiefs of Staff. So, [there is] always a significant reluctance to . . . 'open up' the UCP."[83] Furthermore, David Aaron, who was the Deputy National Security Advisor at the time, recalls that at the time, "the services simply felt that they had standing requirements and priorities that they had to continue to meet and that this was kind of a side show. . . . [T]hey were reluctant to turn around and give high priority to something like this under those circumstances."[84] Faced with the pressure to implement the RDF requirement, however, the Services naturally calculated what their preferred outcome would be.[85]

The Army's position, shared by the Air Force and General David Jones, Chairman of the JCS (CJCS) (who later came around to the Navy/Marine position), was to assign the Middle East, Africa, and South Asia to REDCOM for most normal operations.[86] Since EUCOM had performed well in the Middle East, it should retain control over security assistance programs and minor contingency operations. However, they argued that existing NATO commitments meant that major contingencies would be better handled by REDCOM. The Marines and the Navy, however, wanted to create an RDJTF "administratively within REDCOM, but with operational autonomy to plan, exercise, and deploy to the Persian Gulf region." Operational control would then pass to EUCOM or PACOM once deployed. Strengthening REDCOM by assigning area responsibilities would have been advantageous for the Army, as it was headed by an Army general— and so was EUCOM. As Robert Murray notes, "[T]he Army probably liked Readiness Command because it was a command that was always led by an Army officer."[87] In putting this forward, the Army arguably wanted to strengthen one of the commands led by an Army general without taking core responsibilities away from EUCOM.

In August 1979, the Army appointed a Commander in Chief (CINC), REDCOM, with strong views on the command's role: General Volney Warner saw his mandate as remedying the weakness of U.S. power projection by regaining area responsibilities for his new command, which its predecessor STRICOM had lost at the beginning of the decade. He wanted to "take Readiness Command and walk it backwards to get it into a position where it actually became again Strike Command, given the . . . Russian new-found ability to do rapid deployment of their own."[88] A predicament for the U.S. military was that it "had large parts of the globe for which no unified commander was responsible — that fell directly under the Joint Chiefs of Staff." He adds that, "[j]ust because there's nobody there it's no reason to ignore it because . . . that's where you have your problem." For him, STRICOM "had been born 30 years too soon," and the United States "needed Strike Command as a legitimate, all-Service command . . . rather than Readiness Command whose missions [were] limited to training the forces and had no area responsibility."

The Marines and the Navy thought differently about the RDF requirement: They did not want to see a new constellation that would take away from their core tasks. Hence, the Marines and the Navy did not like the idea of a STRICOM-like structure. As Warner notes, "STRICOM was anathema to the Navy and the Marine Corps. They didn't want to hear about it." Assignment of the Persian Gulf region to REDCOM was unacceptable to them. More fundamentally, the quarrel was about the fear that a strengthened REDCOM would intrude into what the Marines saw as part of their core tasks: rapid deployment. In Warner's view, these discussions were "still a spill-over from World War II" because, in a sense, there already existed two rapid deployment forces: 18th Airborne Corps delivered by the Air Force, and the Marine Corps delivered by the Navy. From his perspective at the time, "the Marines were very concerned [about] creating [the RDJTF] underneath an Army commander . . . which would more or less anoint that command with what they presumed to be their previous role." In other words, "they were really worried about losing their predominance as the . . . expeditionary force." Indeed, when STRICOM first had gained area responsibilities in 1962-63, General David Shoup, Commandant of the Marine Corps, had feared that it would lead to the creation of a "world-wide General Purpose Forces Command."[89] A November 1979 briefing sheet for Jones noted that the Navy and the Marines "did not agree that a distinct entity identified as 'The Rapid Deployment Force' should be established," and they "objected to [the] implicit requirement that all Services assign forces to the JTF [Joint Task Force]."[90] Also, the Marines wanted to link "RDJTF composition . . . to a specific region or contingency."

The Navy had its own separate reasons for supporting the Marine Corps position. They felt that they were already operationally deployed to the area, and therefore there was no need to submit their forces to a joint undertaking, especially in merely providing strategic lift. Warner argues that "the Chief of Naval Operations was the only one of the Chiefs who had an operational responsibility for the Navy. So, it was very difficult to bring them on board, since they didn't want to be brought on board."[91]

In sum, the service quarrel revolved largely around the rivalry over organizational responsibilities, which put the Army and the Marine Corps at odds. As Warner argues, it "came up against the issue of the expeditionary force, the amphibious nature of the Marine Corps, and the roles-and-missions issue. . . . And all of those Service interests were extremely difficult to sort out."

The NSC staff entered the discussion on July 9, 1979, when Brzezinski asked Brown to submit an update on the RDF.[92] The NSC staff — Odom in particular — soon emerged as strong advocates of a unified command as part of a new security framework for the Persian Gulf. Odom saw a unified command as "a major 'next step',"[93] as a unified command would not just mean "bureaucratic re-shuffling." Anticipating strong reactions in the military, he noted that the people, "who know the significance of the UCP, will express very pro and very con views, depending on where they sit in Defense." He told Brzezinski that changing the UCP was under consideration in some parts of the DoD, but it was unlikely to make its way to the policy level unless Brzezinski asked for it.

In fact, Odom had always wondered why the U.S. commands ". . . operations in the Persian Gulf and Middle East through Stuttgart and Brussels, i.e., through SACEUR [the Supreme Allied Commander Europe] and his U.S. staff at EUCOM, [a staff which] focus[es] primarily on the Warsaw Pact and Northern Europe."[94] He argued that a unified command would increase U.S. capabilities in the region, as "such an organizational change would put you and the President in a better position to coordinate the agencies' efforts in the region, and most important, it increases our operational capabilities for the future." A unified command would underline renewed regional commitment because it would be able to project forces and build up local defenses. Also, it would provide a regional focus, as the United States tended, "through State and CIA, to look at the Persian Gulf region country-by-country, embassy-by-embassy." Odom thus suggested that they could "start with a JTF commanded by a major general, a modest arrangement, and let it evolve into a 'Unified Command' requiring a change in the UCP. Or we could start with a Unified Command located in the United States but very thin and austere in staff and capabilities."

He judged that they were up against major interests. He argued that General Jones would not like it because it would take away power from his office (which probably overstated the Chairman's stakes in the issue).[95] Misperceiving service interests, he argued that the Service chiefs would favor it strongly, especially the Army and the Navy ones.[96] The State Department would oppose it because it might

> take the actions away from the embassies and the State country desks. It tends to force a strategic view of our policy and capabilities much broader than 'diplomacy' on a bilateral basis. Defense and CIA will be seen as 'taking over' what is justly State's territory.

The CIA, he judged, would ultimately go along. He could not predict Secretary Brown's position, as he probably did "not have one and will not until forced to have one." However, when Odom first recommended a unified command two other NSC staffers opposed it and Brzezinski put it aside for the time being.[97] Odom remained steadfast, however, and kept pushing the issue because he believed that it was "the best thing we can do to cope with the uncertainties of the future in the region."[98]

When Brown sent Brzezinski a response to the memo of July 9, "the President noted that he did not see that much progress has been made."[99] Brzezinski forwarded this to Brown in another memo and asked for a more in-depth report. According to Odom, it was these two NSC staff requests that "caused the first real interest in doing something about building new capabilities for the Persian Gulf Region" in the DoD.

In Brown's next and more in-depth memorandum on August 16, he argued that modest progress regarding the RDF had been made.[100] However, a report accompanying Brown's reply noted that "it takes several years to institute programs and bring them to fruition" and went on to say that the steps taken in response to the RDF requirement since August 1977 were "just now beginning to take effect, and most of our work is before us." Thus, any contingency that would have required heavy forces could only be resolved "by impinging on our planned capability to reinforce NATO." When Brzezinski forwarded Brown's report to the President, Brzezinski highlighted the need for clearly defined goals in the Persian Gulf.[101] He would therefore "begin a dialogue with Harold to first, better define such a framework, and then, to refine the forces appropriate to our strategy."

After the U.S. Embassy in Tehran was stormed in November of 1979, Odom again weighed in and underlined that a unified command would increase U.S. military capabilities.[102] He was disappointed by the progress, however. While Brzezinski had "generated very great pressure within Defense to do something about it," he was "impressed, thus far, by the failure of Defense to take advantage of the RDF for improving our doctrine and general purpose force structure." It was "a chance to solve a number of strategic lift issues" and "an opportunity to force the Army and the Marines to become more effective." He also argued that the Gulf had become the "forward edge of the battle area," making a unified command a necessity.[103] While he saw the JCS dragging their feet, the DoD had begun to consider the issue, but he did not believe that "we will get movement unless you [Brzezinski] and Harold Brown take the lead."[104]

In these delicate discussions, the DoD was caught between the Services on the one hand and the NSC staff on the other. They thus sought a compromise solution. Nevertheless, the political level in the DoD did have an idea that the RDJTF would only be an initial step on the way to a unified command. Brown thus argues that "there's always an argument about command arrangements. And what we came up with was a compromise, really — recognizing that things would evolve."[105] He also recalls that "I think *I* always had the intention that it would become a separate command."[106] Murray argues similarly that they were trying to get things moving fast to put something together "within the reasonably near term that would actually be able to work and that could actually start work."[107] Shoemaker indeed argues that Murray, under whom he worked at the time, wanted "to have some organization — some command — that owned up and was responsible for the region," but he "could not get a senior consensus. So the next best thing was to establish a joint task force."[108] For Murray, the RDJTF under REDCOM in Florida was thus a logical first step "because that was the only place that actually had facilities and communications equipment."[109]

Brown concurs: "You had a substantial command in Readiness Command, and it therefore made a certain amount of sense to attach the Rapid Deployment Joint Task Force to it." A command in the Gulf was out of the question because of local sensitivities, but giving REDCOM area responsibilities directly was not a good idea, either. As Murray notes, "They didn't have any expertise or any useful local knowledge that would make them valuable. Moreover, they had a high single-service orientation. So, we invented the RDJTF."[110]

In the end, Brown decided on the compromise RDJTF solution along the lines of Marine/Navy preferences: a subordinate command under REDCOM with substantial autonomy and an initial focus on the Persian Gulf.[111] He instructed the CJCS to set up a US-based JTF "to plan, train, and exercise and to be prepared to deploy and employ, designated forces of the RDF as directed to respond to worldwide contingencies."[112] Thus, on November 29, the JCS created the RDJTF under REDCOM's operational command. In December, they appointed as the first Commander, RDJTF (COMRDJTF), Marine General P. X. Kelley, who would later become Commandant of the Marine Corps under President Reagan. It was to become fully operational on March 1, 1980.

Maybe surprisingly, given Odom's earlier judgment, the State Department remained rather passive in the RDF discussion. However, since the RDF had already been mandated in PD-18, it was arguably more about implementation at this point. Nevertheless, the State Department as a whole did not like the idea of strengthening command arrangements for the Persian Gulf. As Brown notes, "The State Department people, I think, didn't like the whole idea because . . . they tended to see military capability as an alternative to diplomacy."[113] Shoemaker concurs,

Now, the State middle-grade—by middle-grade, I really mean Assistant Secretary-level down—were not in favor of [a unified command] because they felt it represented a militarization of the region and that our goals and objectives could be better achieved through diplomatic means.[114]

However, the middle-level officials could not get back-up against strengthening command arrangements from the Secretaries of State, Cyrus Vance and later Edmund Muskie.[115] In Shoemaker's judgment,

Vance and then Muskie really didn't have strong views either way. Vance recognized the importance of it, but also recognized that his ability to shape the Defense Department's Unified Command Plan was virtually nil. When Muskie came in, he didn't really know the background or issues.[116]

Thus, "the fact that neither Secretary was particularly willing or eager to lead into what was clearly a very contentious issue in the Defense Department essentially took State out of play." Nevertheless, Brown recalls that "I think their attitude was part of the reason that we didn't make a big thing . . . a bigger thing of this—that we, in particular, didn't try to put substantial forces into the region."[117]

In sum, caught between an interservice quarrel and an NSC staff pressing for a unified command, the DoD opted for a compromise solution to get things moving. This compromise, however, would soon create unintended consequences.

FROM THE INVASION OF AFGHANISTAN TO REAGAN'S INAUGURATION

Afghanistan and the Persian Gulf Security Framework.

When the USSR intervened on Christmas of 1979 with about 80,000 soldiers to prop up its allies in Kabul, it presented a major shift in the balance in the Persian Gulf region. It was "an extremely grave challenge" in Brzezinski's eyes: "If the Soviets succeed in Afghanistan, and if Pakistan acquiesces, the age-long dream of Moscow to have direct access to the Indian Ocean will have been fulfilled."[118] The Soviet action posed "a test involving ultimately the balance of power between East and West."[119] To deter similar Soviet actions in the future, Brzezinski believed that a long-term commitment was required which demanded, *inter alia*, strategic modernization, increased defense spending, improvements in NATO, and implementation of the RDF requirement. Western Europe, East Asia, and the Persian Gulf had now become "interdependent central strategic zones."

The Soviet invasion served as the galvanizing event for Brzezinski and the NSC staff to redesign U.S. strategic policy and create the Persian Gulf Security Framework (PGSF), ultimately put to paper in PD-63 on January 15, 1981.[120] However, the path towards the PGSF was like "pulling teeth:"[121] The policy differences were still there, and the State Department, in particular, continued to fight many of the proposed steps. In the end, the NSC staff was successful in convincing the DoD and in sidelining the State Department's objections by taking advantage of crisis management mechanisms, presidential back-up in crucial situations, clear strategic goals and a seemingly ad hoc implementation scheme.[122] The NSC staff was thus able to bypass "the second and third levels in State and Defense," achieving a sharp and rapid turn-around in U.S. policy. The creation of the PGSF, which consisted of a number of military, diplomatic, economic and intelligence actions, cannot be dealt with in detail here (for an overview, see Figure 1).[123] In the context of this paper, it is important to note, however, that the struggle for a unified command was a major part of the effort.

Days before the invasion, David Aaron had received a JCS update on the RDF.[124] Little had happened since Brown's last report of August 16, 1979. The problematic issues were still the right force composition, the fact that many forces were committed to NATO and the RDF at the same time, shortcomings in readiness levels, and the final command arrangements. One factor for the slow implementation, which the JCS emphasized, was that the RDF requirement was new and that it would take "at least 5 years . . . to break the RDF logistic logjam." On command arrangements, Aaron noted that the RDJTF had been approved, but that it had not been resolved who would command it and who would have operational control over it once deployed. While acknowledging the validity of some of the JCS arguments, Aaron still recommended that the NSC staff "should keep the heat on Harold to ensure that Defense makes these difficult bureaucratic decisions soon, so they can get the 'chair-shuffling' behind them and get on with the harder task of formulating specific military objectives and plans for the region."

PERSIAN GULF SECURITY FRAMEWORK
Military Component
• Enhancement of U.S. force capabilities • Development of RDF • Modernization and expansion of strategic air-and sealift • Regional base access • Overbuilding of regional facilities • Prepositioning supplies in the Indian Ocean • Exercises in the region • Increased military presence • Effective command arrangements • Improvement of local defense capabilities
Foreign Policy Component
• Progress in the Middle East Peace Process • Improved security relations with Turkey and Pakistan • Increased security assistance to Saudi Arabia and other friendly Gulf States • Improved ties with Somalia, Djibouti and (if possible) Ethiopia • Increased access and overflight rights to the Persian Gulf • Prevention of pro-Soviet, radicalized or fragmented Iran
Economic Component
• Improved oil policy • Increased Western economic assistance to the region • Increased Saudi and other Gulf states' cooperation in financing of regional security needs • Improved economic stability in the region
Intelligence Component
• Development of an effective, regionally integrated intelligence program

Figure 1. Overview of the Persian Gulf Security Framework.

Commenting on Aaron's memo, Odom noted that Brown had instructed the JCS to look into the UCP to possibly establish a unified command, but that they had "dodged successfully."[125] He did not see the RDJTF as a permanent solution, as its location in Florida did "little to help" the United States in the Gulf. However, he also saw that Brown and Jones were caught between Service interests: Jones "will suffer enormous pressures if he tries to push through a unified command change. Brown also would anger senior military figures in the Services if he forced the UCP change." They were therefore "understandably reluctant to create this internal discontent if they can avoid it." Consequently, he recommended that the NSC staff "take the 'heat' for them by getting the President to send a directive that it be done."

Odom would repeatedly make these arguments during the remainder of the year. Soon, Brzezinski and the President (in principle) adopted this position as well. Consequently, on January 25, Brzezinski asked Brown to take another look at the command plan.[126] Ultimately, however, the Services beat the NSC staff on the issue — a "critical defeat" in Odom's eyes.[127] Just when the DoD started coming around to the objectives of the framework and the State Department "had been brought around, or rendered unable to block the effort, . . . the military was just beginning to build opposition, much more significant and effective."

Whither the Rapid Deployment Joint Task Force?

In late January, Brzezinski asked Brown to reopen the command plan for the Persian Gulf, and service squabbles broke out once again.[128] However, the RDJTF compromise had unintentionally created another layer of interests in the military. The vague formulation of the arrangements enabled both General Kelley, COMRDJTF, and his superior, General Warner, CINC, Readiness Command (CINCRED), to claim control of the RDJTF.

Responding to the renewed pressure, the Marines wanted to let the RDJTF become operational as planned before considering any changes at all. The Army, however, wanted to create both a new unified command and to keep the RDJTF with a reinforced global mission for undesignated areas. Warner himself, doubting that he could handle more than limited contingency operations, recommended strengthening REDCOM and the RDJTF. The JCS as a whole suggested a solution in line with Marine preferences: The RDJTF should come into action as planned, but once deployed, Kelley should become CINC for a unified command in order to avoid organizational complications. Adjusting this recommendation, Secretary Brown informed the President via Aaron on February 5 that the RDJTF would become a subordinate of REDCOM in peacetime, but that in case of deployment the RDJTF would come under the control of EUCOM, PACOM or directly under the National Command Authority (NCA), i.e., the President and the Secretary of Defense.[129] Still, Brown would also analyze the need for a separate command in the coming months, according to Aaron. The RDJTF thus became operational as planned on March 1.

This did not spell the end of the struggle over command arrangements, however. While the NSC staff was pushing for a unified command from above, Warner and Kelley were locked into an argument over who, ultimately, had control of the RDJTF. The DoD had created the command with substantial autonomy in mind, but Warner argued that the fact that he held operational control meant that he should be responsible for planning, training, exercises, and interfacing with the political level. Kelley was of the opposite view.

The strained relationship between Warner and Kelley was seen as highly personal from the outside, but both deny this. Indeed, organizational interests made this conflict almost unavoidable. Given the vague formulation of command arrangements for the RDJTF, both generals had the opportunity to vie for control of the command. In a way, the RDJTF went from something that nobody in the military really wanted to something that everyone was interested in getting a piece of.

Both men had assumed their new jobs with the goal of making the best out of what they perceived as their respective mandates. As Warner notes, "I would argue, when I went there I knew what I wanted to do and I [had] been doing it before and it seemed to all make sense to me. And I think the same was pretty well true with Kelley."[130]

Kelley was intended to be a rather autonomous commander by the DoD, but understandably Warner did not want to give up control, since his objective was trying to strengthen REDCOM. As Murray remembers, "He's trying to make something of his command. And this *is* a thorn in his side."[131] Brown argues similarly:

> Well, it was inevitable that there would be friction, . . . as there always is with a subordinate command. Because a senior commander doesn't like the idea that one of his subordinates has a direct...could have a direct channel. And Kelley, being a gung-ho Marine, was quite willing to try to go around the Readiness Command—and succeeded...enough... He succeeded enough—I'm sure—to annoy Warner, without [*chuckle*] getting everything he wanted.[132]

Furthermore, the Service agendas were superimposed on the REDCOM/RDJTF clash as well, since neither man was free of service interests. As Warner argues, "we were both trying to preserve our own service interest, as we came together as a joint headquarters."[133] In other words, "Kelley can't offend the Commandant of the Marine Corps. I can't offend the Chairman or the Chief of Staff of the Army."

After the first command post exercise of the RDJTF from April 10-15, 1980, an RDJTF staff paper summed up the differences between Warner and Kelley.[134] It noted that command arrangements "specifically task COMRDJTF with the responsibility to plan for rapid deployment forces operations" in the Persian Gulf region. Kelley therefore argued that it was "his specific responsibility to accomplish these plans." Warner countered that he had the operational command, and that it therefore was "ultimately a [REDCOM] responsibility to accomplish that planning." This issue was complicated even more by the fact that REDCOM was prohibited from having area responsibilities under the UCP.

As a result of these differences, Warner protested to Brown about the unclear chain of command. On the one hand, Kelley was under Warner's "operational command for planning, joint training, and exercises." On the other hand, Kelley was tasked "with specific responsibilities outside the jurisdiction of [CINCRED]." In a memo sent to Brown on April 21,[135] Warner thus sought confirmation that "all pre-deployment missions (planning and exercises) and allocations (personnel and dollars) assigned to COMRDJTF are through and subject to [CINCRED]."

Another bone of contention was the Washington Liaison Office, an RDJTF office established to interface

with the policy level in the capital. Murray empha-
sizes the significance that he attributed to the office:

> I was very keen that [Kelley] should have the Wash-
> ington office because the policy action happens in
> Washington . . . — not in Florida. And if you're not in
> touch with what's going on in the policy world you're
> missing a dimension. . . . So if we wanted him to be
> well-clued in and be in the bull's eye of the policy
> world then he had to have sharp ears and have some
> folks up here who were paying attention to what was
> going on.[136]

Warner understandably did not like this arrangement at all, since it provided ample opportunity to bypass his desk. He recalls that "I would find out things
had been decided and happened that went directly
down to the other end of the runway, which didn't
please me a hell of a lot. Having been in charge, I like
the chain of command."[137] In a comment to the JCS on
proposed changes to RDJTF arrangements, Warner
argued that he was barred "from most essential task-
ings and in my ability to direct the [Headquarters of
the] RDJTF to do anything other than what has been
directed by JCS or [the NCA]."[138]

Equally understandably, Kelley liked the Washington Liaison Office and wanted to keep it.[139] He also
wanted to avoid increased control by Warner, since "a
total subjugation of the RDJTF under REDCOM could
transmit a 'signal' that the stature and importance
of the RDJTF are already on the wane — only three
months after activation." Hence he suggested that

> if we desire to transmit a strong and positive signal of
> our intentions and resolve in the Middle East/Persian
> Gulf, it should not be obfuscated in a conventional bu-
> reaucratic hierarchy — it must be highly visible, with
> sufficient clarity for all to see!

On May 6, not long after—in Odom's words—"General Warner's devastating reclama to the JCS and Harold Brown" and the failed rescue of the U.S. hostages in Iran, Odom suggested a way to proceed on the RDJTF.[140] He argued that the first RDJTF exercise, the rescue mission, and some of Kelley's instructions indicated "confusion, misunderstandings, and inadequacies on the command arrangements." He thus wanted Brzezinski "to strike quickly," because time was running out "to get either the operational advantages or the political advantages of the command change."

However, Odom was still too optimistic about establishing a separate command. Commenting on progress on the Persian Gulf Security Framework on May 12, he complained that the United States was "essentially blocked in many of the security framework endeavors for lack of an independent command for the region."[141] He had learned "that things are far more confused and complex than even I had suspected." Not only did REDCOM and the RDJTF want to plan for the Persian Gulf, but EUCOM and PACOM had entered the discussions as well, arguing that the RDJTF should be made a subordinate command under either one of them.[142] Odom still saw a unified command as the linchpin for a new U.S. strategy in the Gulf:

> Unless the President orders Brown and Jones to establish a separate regional unified command for the Persian Gulf and Indian Ocean, we are going nowhere on deployments, exercises, and contingency planning, not to mention the management of 'local defense' and [Foreign Military Sales] in a fashion to our advantage.[143]

On July 25, the JCS sent another proposal for changes to Brown.[144] They argued that "there is a need to focus the mission of the RDJTF exclusively on [Southwest Asian] contingencies" and that Warner should maintain operational command over the RDJTF "for all predeployment planning, training, exercises, and preparation for employment." The Marines, however, dissented and wanted the RDJTF to be "a separate and distinct planning element directly under the JCS." The JCS recommendations were adopted, and Warner thus strengthened his position.[145]

However, the belated implementation of the RDF requirement and the continuing squabbles would become a liability in 1980, as Carter had vowed in his State of the Union Address to repel any meddling by the Soviets in the Gulf.

The Soviet Military Threat in the Gulf.

While the senior policymaking level was trying to devise and implement a new strategy for the Gulf, intelligence reports were making the administration increasingly anxious that the USSR could exploit the power vacuum in the region and would press on from their newly-won position in Afghanistan. Consequently, the wide gap between the commitment made in the Carter Doctrine and the actual military capabilities in the region was revealed: The United States would have been unable to defend Iran. In a sense, the United States was punished for acting too late on the RDF. While this dire situation provided further thrust in the NSC staff for a unified command, it was still not successful in overcoming the organizational interests in the end. The whole episode of the Soviet military threat to Iran can unfortunately not be told here (see Figure 2).[146] Here, it is important to show that the inability to deal with a possible invasion of Iran demonstrated the risks incurred by delayed implementation of the RDF requirement. It has to be kept in mind, however, that even a perfect implementation process would only have improved the situation slightly — the loss of Iran as an ally was simply too momentous and unanticipated.[147]

SOVIET MILITARY THREAT TO IRAN	
Christmas 1979	Soviet invasion of Afghanistan
January 1980	First unusual Soviet activities in the Transcaucasus and North Caucasus
January 15, 1980	First CIA paper on Soviet intentions regarding Iran
January 23, 1980	State of the Union Address (Carter Doctrine)
January 29, 1980	Second CIA paper on Soviet intentions regarding Iran
April 1980	Advancing, but still low-cost preparatory measures in the Transcaucasus
August 8, 1980	Third CIA paper on Soviet intentions regarding Iran
Mid-August	U.S. gains intelligence on Soviet exercise in the Transcaucasus
August 22, 1980	Senior discussion on whether a Soviet invasion could occur within the next year (CIA and State Department papers)
September 2, 1980	Senior discussion on U.S. military options in Iran/Persian Gulf (JCS paper) • Preparation of intelligence briefings for NATO and regional allies tasked • Working group established for Muskie-Gromyko meeting (talking points and nonpaper) • DoD tasked to further review possible defense actions and horizontal escalation
September 5, 1980	Senior discussion on non-paper for Muskie-Gromyko meeting

Figure 2. Timeline of the Soviet Military
Threat to Iran.

September 12, 1980	NSC meeting • West Germany, France, and the UK to be approached (and talking points revised accordingly) • DoD tasked to continue to plan and prepare military steps regarding horizontal escalation and defensive operations in Iran • NATO, Asian and regional allies to be briefed
September 22, 1980	Iraq attacks Iran
September 25, 1980	Muskie-Gromyko meeting at United Nations General Assembly
November 11, 1980	DoD paper on military implications of Iraq-Iran war on defensive plans for Iran
December 12, 1980	NSC meeting on PD-62 and PD-63
January 15, 1980	PD-62 ("Modifications in U.S. National Strategy") and PD-63 ("Persian Gulf Security Framework") issued

Figure 2. Timeline of the Soviet Military Threat to Iran. (Cont.)

In early 1980, the CIA did not doubt that the USSR wanted to improve its regional influence, but it also considered it unlikely "that the Soviet occupation of Afghanistan will turn out to have been a dress rehearsal for an impending gala performance in Iran."[148] However, throughout the spring, the United States received intelligence of mobilization exercises and other unusual activities by Soviet forces in the Transcaucasus bordering Northwest Iran, which "further heightened concerns that the Soviets may have aggressive intentions toward that country." Still, the CIA did not see activities that indicated impending invasion and cautioned that the USSR most likely recognized that an "attempt to seize the entire country would run a high risk of direct confrontation with the United States."[149]

Further intelligence data of advancing preparatory measures prompted an alternative intelligence interpretation in a CIA study on August 8, however. The normal view was still "that the Soviets are planning in a routine way for unexpected contingencies," but the study examined the possibility "that the Soviets have embarked on a course of action which may portend an invasion of Iran." The CIA thus argued that "Soviet resort to its evolving military option against Iran would represent a move undertaken in the confidence that a worthy opportunity was at hand, one that affected overall Soviet concerns enough to justify potentially high cost and substantial risk."

Consequently, the next meeting on the PGSF revolved around the question of "whether a Soviet attack toward the Gulf could materialize within the next year."[150] The CIA noted that the USSR was "taking steps to strengthen the ability of its forces to invade Iran, should Soviet leaders so decide," but also that "the Soviets have not made a decision to invade Iran. At least during the next several months."[151] A low-risk opportunity and a U.S. military intervention were judged to be the most likely precipitating factors for a Soviet invasion. The CIA, the DoD, and the State Department seemed to suggest that the odds for a Soviet attack were one in 10 or 20, but one unknown pessimist on the NSC staff saw them closer to one in three or five.[152]

In mid-August, the United States gained access to Soviet exercise data from the Transcaucasus through intelligence channels. In Warner's words, this "caused a great deal of excitement all over the Washington area, as to whether or not [the Soviets] were serious and might close down the Strait [of Hormuz] and make a move on the Middle East."[153] Much remains classified, but the basic elements of the crisis can be gathered from subsequent discussions. Jones argued that "the planned operations were not for limited territorial control such as would be characteristic of an intervention to quiet down a chaotic or destabilized Iran, but rather it seems that the Soviets have a master plan for seizing the oil-bearing region."[154] He even suggested that weather conditions could encourage invasion in the fall of 1980. According to him, the exercise consisted of three phases: "Phase I, occupation of northwest Iran (2-3 weeks); Phase II, consolidation and logistics buildup (3-4 weeks); and Phase III, operations to the south through Iran and Iraq to capture the oil-bearing regions of the Arabian peninsula (5-6 weeks)." Brzezinski judged that "the politically logical sequence is to do Phase I, hope that the United States would not take any effective military response, expect that if we do not it will lead to a demoralization of Iran which will, in turn, facilitate Phase II and Phase III." In other words, they judged that the United States was in serious trouble.

To recall the Carter Doctrine, the United States had committed itself to the defense of the Persian Gulf against outside aggression: An assault on the Gulf would "be repelled by any means necessary, including military force."[155] The problem was that the United States did not yet have the capabilities and command arrangements in place to make good on that promise.

Even before the August exercise, it had become clear that the United States could not defend Iran against a full-scale Soviet assault.[156] Two other options were seen as more promising, but still risky: defense of Iranian oil fields in the south and a broader Persian Gulf strategy that would primarily defend Saudi oil. The JCS were subsequently tasked to prepare a paper on these military options.[157] The simple conclusion was that the United States "cannot win any confrontation with the Soviets in the region if the Soviets are not deterred from using their large conventional advantage."[158] Odom believed that the JCS were "deeply disturbed." However, he pointed out that "[t]his kind of showdown was inevitable. We have been driving toward it since last summer and your memos to Brown on the RDF."[159]

The still classified JCS paper confirmed the grim situation: "Currently deployed and rapidly deployable U.S. forces now available are judged to have very limited, but still not zero deterrent value."[160] The overall assessment of the military situation was this:

> At present, were the Soviets to begin mobilizing forces to invade Iran, the United States could use the approximately one month of warning to close on the Persian Gulf 1 [and] 1/3 divisions, 3 carrier battle groups . . ., and about 7 tactical fighter squadrons . . . , all with very lean support. In the same time, Soviets could close on Iran some 16-20 fully manned divisions and some 450 combat aircraft, enough to advance to the Gulf.[161]

Consequently, Jones underlined that none of the three proposed military options "can stop a Soviet invasion of the 16-20 divisions," and that the United States could not "defend Iran on any line today against a determined Soviet attack."[162] The question then became how to deter a Soviet invasion, while being unable to defend Iran if deterrence failed. The senior policymakers on the SCC came to this dire conclusion:

> In spreading the conflict geographically, i.e. 'horizontal escalation' as opposed to 'vertical escalation' with nuclear weapons, it was agreed that the Soviets have

nothing abroad that we could take which equals in importance to them what Iran and the oil producing regions in the Gulf are to the United States and its allies.[163]

The President would therefore later judge that the Soviets were "sure that they can prevail militarily unless the United States uses nuclear weapons," and he saw "no way for a Soviet invasion of Iran to not become a worldwide confrontation."[164] His senior Advisors had agreed earlier that "if the Soviets succeeded in the Persian Gulf region, Western Europe's freedom from the Soviet Union would be lost."[165]

Making the whole issue even more complicated was the danger of the United States itself triggering a Soviet invasion. As the State Department had already pointed out, deterrence via credible threats and preparatory military steps was "in tension with a coequal objective of not precipitating the very military action which we seek to deter."[166]

At the center of U.S. efforts to make clear to the Soviets that the United States would respond militarily to an invasion was a meeting between Edmund Muskie and the Soviet Foreign Minister Andrei Gromyko at the United Nations (UN). At the meeting on September 25, a non-paper, over which heated debates between senior policymakers took place, was given to Gromyko. It stated that "[a]ny military attempt to gain control of the Persian Gulf area, including specifically Soviet military action in Iran, could lead to a direct military confrontation with the U.S."[167] No declassified documents are available yet that describe the Soviet reaction to this move.[168] It is fortunate that the Soviets did not choose to invade Iran, given the fact that the United States would have been faced with the fateful decision whether to accept defeat or employ tactical nuclear weapons against Soviet troops, a scenario that could have precipitated a very dangerous spiral of escalation.

While the situation eventually led to PD-62 and PD-63 to strengthen the U.S. position vis-à-vis the USSR, the NSC staff could still not get the President or the Secretary of Defense to mandate a unified command for the Persian Gulf. Shoemaker describes the impact of the Soviet threat on command arrangements:

> From the White House perspective, it got Brzezinski to say to Odom: We have got to get on with this now. Over in the Pentagon, it was more complex because it certainly elevated the importance of the RDJTF, but it also reinforced the squabbling going on and sometimes you can get things done quietly that you can't get done, when the spotlight is on that particular area. So, it's not altogether surprising that even though intuitively you would say that 'Boy, this must have really got them fired up to solve the problem.' In reality, it got everybody fired up and in some ways intensified the problem.[169]

The question remains, of course, why the President did not use his formal authority to order the establishment of a unified command. Here, Shoemaker argues that Carter:

> was very willing to listen to views. He was much less willing to make contentious decisions that perhaps in his heart he did not necessarily believe in—I don't know if that's true. . . . He was not at all convinced that military power was the way to address problems in the region. And we took this to him. And he would consistently say 'Well, let's see if we can't get the Joint Chiefs aboard.' and 'No, I'm not ready to make that mandate yet.' And then by the time November rolled around. . . .

Actually by the time October rolled around, it was apparent that there wasn't going to be a second term. He sort of gave up.[170]

This episode shows that the United States was punished for not taking seriously the establishment of an RDF that had already been mandated in 1977. Still, we have to keep in mind that even prompt RDF implementation would not have made up for the loss of Iran. Also, it would not have prevented the two events that changed the balance of power in the region fundamentally. As Secretary Brown asks rhetorically, "Would it have prevented the Iranian revolution? No. Would it have changed Soviet behavior, prevented them from invading Afghanistan? I don't see how."[171]

EPILOGUE: THE REAGAN ADMINISTRATION AND CENTRAL COMMAND

By the end of the Carter administration, a fundamental shift in U.S. strategy towards the Persian Gulf had occurred, but the wish of the NSC staff to create a unified command was left unfulfilled. On February 11, 1981, General Odom—now the Assistant Chief of Staff for Intelligence in the Army—sent a memo to Reagan's National Security Advisor, Richard Allen, where he described the process that led to the Persian Gulf Security Framework.[172] While he traced its beginnings to PRM-10, he also recounted the difficulties that the NSC faced in shifting policy priorities in the early years:

The combination of the PD-13 arms transfer policy, Indian Oceans Arms Talks, non-proliferation and improper application of the human rights policy, intersected in the Persian Gulf region in a most unfavorable fashion for U.S. interests. We fought a three-year battle to de-emphasize those policies in that region and to face up to the military security requirements there. Events in November and December 1979 reduced State's resistance—as well as that of the military services—and we began an integrated approach to building a security framework.[173]

He emphasized that the new administration should not veer from its course. Taking it apart would only make sense "if you intend to abandon the region and beat a strategic retreat." Regarding a unified command, he argued that the President should take the lead:

> Our own military command and control for the region is in shambles, and the JCS is institutionally incapable of improving it. The inter-service quarrels, particularly on the 'Unified Command Plan,' are paralyzing. The big ones will not be settled without direct orders from the President which are delivered in unambiguous words.[174]

Regarding a unified command, Shoemaker, who continued on the NSC staff for another 1 ½ years, recounts that the early months of the new administration were "a perfect time for a message that says: 'Mr. President, this is something that the Carter administration just couldn't get done because it was too weak and too inept and this [is] the kind of thing the American people expect of a strong President'."[175] He was charged with reviewing Carter's PDs, and his memo on PD-63 reached the President. In his words, Reagan "signed on early to the idea of a unified command. For him, it was almost a no-brainer."

Thus, on April 24, 1981, the new Secretary of Defense, Caspar Weinberger, told the JCS "to submit a plan for transformation of the RDJTF within three to five years or less into a 'separate unified command'."[176] After a brief review, they came up with a plan of transitioning into a unified command on January 1, 1983. Despite the early commitment, however, the road to CENTCOM was still rocky and included a last-minute Navy/Marine attempt "to divert the RDJTF from its transition to a unified command." This story cannot be told here, but has to wait until more documents on Reagan's approach to the Persian Gulf become available.

CONCLUSION AND PERSPECTIVES

This paper has examined the story of the RDJTF as an important element in the U.S. strategic turn towards the Persian Gulf that continues to this day. As the direct precursor of CENTCOM, focusing a new command on the Persian Gulf was the beginning of a more in-depth and strategic engagement with this crucial region of global energy and security politics. This last section first briefly summarizes the developments that led to the creation of the RDJTF under Carter. Then, the argument is made that, while the RDJTF episode is a historical case, the underlying challenges of adapting the U.S. national security apparatus to the geostrategic environment have not changed. The paper thus suggests how national security reforms can be understood more generally and calls for further case studies. It concludes with a brief assessment of the national security system today and offers some perspectives going forward.

THE CARTER YEARS AND MILITARY COMMAND ARRANGEMENTS FOR THE PERSIAN GULF

The story of changing command arrangements for the Persian Gulf during the Carter administration falls into three phases. First, soon after Carter's inauguration and as a result of the Comprehensive Net Assessment, the administration recognized major negative trends in the global military balance between the Eastern and Western blocs. One of these developing imbalances was a comparative weakness of U.S. power projection capabilities, especially in the Persian Gulf and Northeast Asia. Consequently, already in 1977, President Carter mandated the establishment of an RDF. However, even though the regional balance was already shifting — to the detriment of the United States and its friends — the DoD and the military Services saw no gains to be made in establishing such a force and, for all intents and purposes, avoided dealing with it. In addition, a split at the policymaking level over how to react to Soviet actions in the Horn of Africa, Yemen, and Afghanistan, as well as the administration's focus on other foreign policy and defense issues, provided additional cover for the military to ignore the RDF.

Second, with the exit of the Shah of Iran in early 1979, the United States lost a key ally in the Persian Gulf, and its regional strategy was in shambles. This led to the first steps towards a new security framework in the Gulf, and the NSC staff pushed for the RDF. Under pressure to come up with a solution, the military became locked into an intense interservice quarrel that pitted the Army, which saw an opportunity to strengthen one of its weaker commands — REDCOM — against the Marine Corps, which saw the RDF as an intrusion into its core task of deploying troops worldwide on short notice. With the DoD lodged between the NSC staff (and thus by implication the President) and the military Services, it devised the RDJTF as a compromise to push things forward. Meanwhile, the NSC staff, with General Odom at the forefront, began to develop a great interest in setting up a unified command.

Third, with the Soviet invasion of Afghanistan in late 1979, the military balance in the Gulf further turned against the United States as Soviet troops drew much closer to the region's center of gravity. The NSC staff, again mostly under Odom's guidance, devised the PGSF in response. Among its proposed elements was the establishment of a unified command. With all eyes on the region, Service interests entered the process again, however, and were joined by another layer of interests, since the RDJTF compromise had produced an unanticipated struggle over control between its commander and his superior, CINCRED. While the costs of failing to set up the RDF earlier became clear, when a serious Soviet military threat to Iran emerged in the summer of 1980, neither the DoD nor the President intervened in this gridlock and no unified command was established in the last year of Carter's presidency. Thus, the creation of CENTCOM had to wait until President Reagan took office.

A HISTORIC CASE, ENDURING CHALLENGES

This paper is concerned with a historic case of reshuffling military command arrangements. Since the military and the national security apparatus have changed so substantially since the days of President Carter, one could argue that it is hardly worthwhile to examine the RDJTF in light of today's challenges to the system of national security in the United States. This view is mistaken.

It is true that the military and the whole national security system look very different today than they did 30 years ago. The Goldwater-Nichols Act of 1986, for example, fundamentally changed the organization of the DoD and the military Services by *inter alia* clarifying chains of command and strengthening incentives to think more jointly about national security. However, the argument here is that the underlying logic of national security reform efforts has not changed, and will in fact not change, at least in its fundamental dynamics.

In a perfect world, the United States would perceive or even anticipate new developments on the world stage correctly and reform its organizations accordingly. Unfortunately, the history of U.S. national security does not support this.[177] In fact, this should not come as much of a surprise, for national security reform processes can arguably be thought of as being subjected to two logics that often—if not always—are at odds.[178] On the one hand, policymakers responsible for foreign and security policy at the top of the administration should be able to perceive changes in the international security environment that would undermine the effectiveness of a certain organizational setup. These officials should therefore pursue organizational reforms to remedy this. After all, these policymakers—whether it be the President himself, his National Security Advisor, or any other principal—can tap into all of the privileged information that the U.S. Government is privy to. For no one else is better "equipped to perceive systemic constraints and deduce the national interest."[179]

On the other hand, however, decisionmakers at the top are almost never omnipotent masters who can reorganize the national security system at their will: In reform processes, they meet bureaucratic players who also have a vast interest in shaping or, indeed, disrupting reforms, and who are the ones having to implement them. Such bureaucrats[180] are representatives of organizations that are to a large degree organizations like any other: They covet increased autonomy from their political superiors and seek larger shares of the budget.[181] In other words, they pursue the particular interest of their respective organizations (and not surprisingly, they most often are convinced that more autonomy and money for their organization is the best option to advance the national interest). For an overview of these two logics at work, see Figure 3 below.

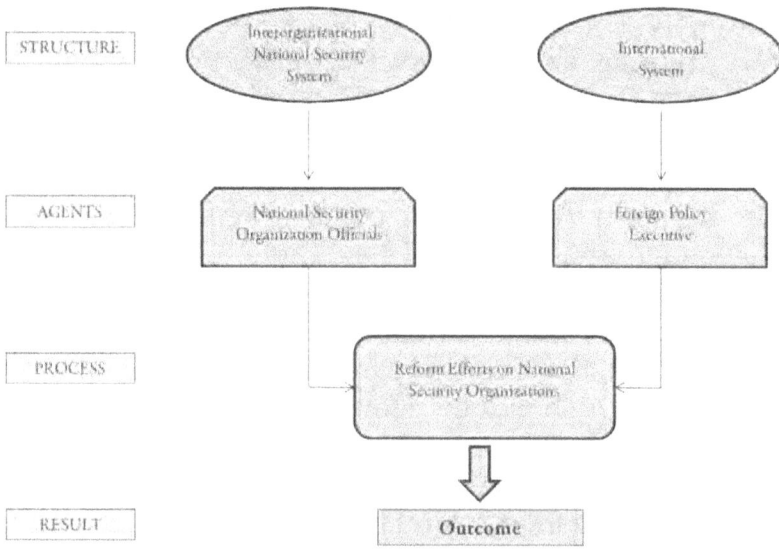

Figure 3. The Policy Process on National Security Organization Reforms.

Pursuing an organization's interest is also made easier by the fact that it proves tricky for senior policymakers to recognize how to respond to changes at the international level. In fact, the imperatives of the international system are rather murky and difficult to read: Misperception is always a possibility, and even if a threat or opportunity is identified correctly, it is sometimes not clear what the optimal response should be.

Bureaucrats not only have the incentives to pursue organizational interests—after all, "Promotion to higher rungs is dependent on years of demonstrated, distinguished devotion to a service's mission"[182]—but they also have the means to do so because of:

- asymmetrical expertise and information,
- the ability to shape the implementation process,
- the ability of drawing on support from outside the administration,
- the ability to portray themselves as apolitical and neutral,
- the ability to play for time, and
- knowledge of their core tasks that have to be protected.

Organizational theory has identified actions that organizations normally pursue or avoid in order to increase—or at least preserve—their autonomy and relative shares of the budget:

- They pursue policies that are most likely to make them more important in the future.
- They seek to protect those capabilities that are crucial for carrying out what they perceive as their core tasks.

- They resist efforts that could weaken the importance of their core tasks or their ability to carry them out.
- They try to rid themselves of tasks they deem nonessential.

Of course, an administration is not totally helpless against seemingly all-powerful bureaucrats: It can reward or punish organizations by increasing or reducing their autonomy or budgetary shares, and most importantly, it has the formal and legitimate authority to tell them what to do. However, these instruments of persuasion tend to be much blunter than they might seem, drain the political capital of an administration, and distract from other policy issues.

Seen in this light, the story of the RDJTF becomes much clearer. First, the changes in the international security environment, in particular in the Persian Gulf, led the Carter administration, first and foremost Brzezinski and Odom, to press for a reform of military arrangements to deal with these new challenges. The decision to establish the RDF was thus made in recognition of negative trends in power projection capabilities. The (delayed) implementation, in the form of the RDJTF, was also driven by further events in the region.

Second, organizational interests in the military delayed and shaped the implementation of the RDF requirement. The military Services ignored the RDF for about 2 years because no one saw benefits for themselves in tackling the issue. When the political level demanded more action in the wake of the Iranian Revolution and the Soviet invasion of Afghanistan, the Services tried to shape the RDJTF compromise according to their organizational interests, now that they could no longer pursue the status quo.

Third, possibly reflecting a mix between organizational interests and misperception of the international security environment, the policy differences at the top about how to react to Soviet assertiveness in the Persian Gulf shows that it often is not clear what the necessary organizational changes should look like, even if changes at the international level are indeed recognized.

Put in these terms, the case of the RDJTF does not look exceptional to those who are familiar with reforms of the U.S. national security system. But much remains to be understood before reforms can be carried out efficiently.

WHERE WE ARE TODAY: THE STATE OF THE U.S. NATIONAL SECURITY SYSTEM

The development of the RDJTF under President Carter provides an example of the difficulties of organizational change in the U.S. national security system. It has been argued that the underlying logic of reforms has not changed: Organizational politics is still the same as it ever was, as organizations pursue their particular interests—sometimes overlapping with the national interest, oftentimes not.

This paper started by suggesting that the U.S. national security system is at a crossroads: The current system, which still rests on the National Security Act of 1947, has not been altered in a way that makes it institutionally capable of tackling the challenges of today and tomorrow. The PNSR's report, *Forging a New Shield*—probably the most comprehensive study on the U.S. national security system to date—argues that "[t]he legacy structures and processes of a national security system that is now more than 60 years old no longer help American leaders to formulate coherent national strategy."[183] The United States generally puts great trust in the ability of individual leaders to prevail over institutional barriers, but it seems that even the brightest leaders can no longer consistently overcome these challenges. The key problems, according to the report, are:

- "The system is grossly imbalanced. It supports strong departmental capabilities at the expense of integrating mechanisms."
- "Resources allocated to departments and agencies are shaped by their narrowly defined core mandates rather than broader national missions."
- "The need for presidential integration to compensate for the systemic inability to adequately integrate or resource missions overly centralizes issue management and overburdens the White House."
- "A burdened White House cannot manage the national security system as a whole to be agile and collaborative at any time, but it is particularly vulnerable to breakdown during the protracted transition periods between administrations."
- "Congress provides resources and conducts oversight in ways that reinforce the first four problems and make improving performance extremely difficult."

On this background, the report identifies the fundamental shortcoming of the system: "[P]arochial departmental and agency interests, reinforced by Congress, paralyze interagency cooperation even as the variety, speed, and complexity of emerging security issues prevent the White House from effectively controlling the system." The report provides a large and detailed package of reforms to remedy these deficiencies. However, if reform processes really are lodged between two often competing logics, as this paper has argued and the analysis of the RDJTF supports — with senior policy makers pursuing the national interest and organizational players pursuing organizational interests — then altering the national security system in such a fundamental way as the PNSR advocates will be exceptionally hard. The case of the RDJTF shows that the same problems that hinder coherent analysis, planning, and implementation of **policies**[184] also create enormous barriers for coherent analysis, planning, and implementation of **organizational reform**. Indeed, changing an organization's structure is probably even harder than changing policies: To change foreign and security policies means changing what an organization **does**; to change organizational structures mean changing what it **is**. Hence, the incentives for bureaucrats to shape or even obstruct reforms are that much greater.

That being said, organizational change for the better is not impossible. In a sense, while not perfect, the passing of the Goldwater-Nichols Act has been an example that stands out, as it made up for decades of organizational inertia in the military. Also, the recent creation of U.S. Africa Command — as a response to lessons learned in how the United States deals with the African continent, disappointing interagency coordination, and the new security challenges of a post-Cold War and post-9/11 world — appears to offer a positive example, regardless of the dismal start-up phase.[185] However, even in this case, it has been alleged that the DoD set up the new command as a way to expand its reach over U.S. Africa policy. Reportedly, the State Department and the U.S. Agency for International Development (USAID) have been dissatisfied with what they see as overreach of the military and the DoD and a possible militarization of U.S. policy on the continent.[186] Thus, it appears that organizational politics is here to stay. Therefore, we must invest much more time and effort into the study of how national security reform processes unfold, in order to gain lessons on how to structure the processes rightly and get a result that more closely reflects the national interest, instead of being the result of organizational bargaining. Ultimately, changes must take place throughout the U.S. national security apparatus, but this is much easier said than done. It will indeed be very difficult to get the national security system to change, but it must happen. Certainly, U.S. administrations are not powerless in reform processes, but they need a better understanding to get what they want and what the security of the nation requires.

ENDNOTES

1. This paper is based upon the author's M.Sc. thesis in Political Science at the University of Copenhagen, Denmark, entitled *Reforming National Security Organizations: US Military Command Arrangements for the Persian Gulf, 1977-1981*, and written under the auspices of the Royal Danish Defence College. It can be obtained directly from the author (*Henrik.Bliddal@gmx.net*) or from the Royal Danish Library, Copenhagen, Denmark.

2. Brzezinski to Carter, February 26, 1977, Memorandum, NSC Weekly Report No. 2, Jimmy Carter Library (hereafter: JCL), *Zbigniew Brzezinski Collection*, Weekly Reports, Box 41, "Weekly Reports 1-15" folder.

3. Jimmy Carter, "State of the Union Address 1980," January 23, 1980, available from *www.jimmycarterlibrary.org/documents/speeches/su80jec.phtml*.

4. The "arc of crisis" was a term coined by Brzezinski in December 1978 in response to the troubles on the horizon in the region.

5. Olav Njølstad, "Shifting Priorities: The Persian Gulf in US Strategic Planning in the Carter Years," *Cold War History*, Vol. 4, No. 3, 2004, p. 22.

6. The two most recent—and best—articles on the RDJTF are Njølstad, "Shifting Priorities,"and William E. Odom, "The Cold War Origins of the U.S. Central Command," *Journal of Cold War Studies*, Vol. 8, No. 2, 2006.

7. For a recent exchange between Walter Russell Mead, Carter, and Brzezinski, see Walter Russell Mead, "The Carter Syndrome," *Foreign Policy*, January/February 2010; and Jimmy Carter, Zbigniew Brzezinski, and Walter Russell Mead, "Presidential Debate," *Foreign Policy*, March/April 2010.

8. Odom, "The Cold War Origins of the U.S. Central Command," p. 53.

9. Njolstad, p. 21.

10. Odom, "The Cold War Origins of the U.S. Central Command," p. 53.

11. Research was conducted at the Headquarters of Central Command, Jimmy Carter Library, Library of Congress, National Archives and Record Administration, National Defense University, and National Security Archives. Interviews were conducted with Harold Brown, Zbigniew Brzezinski, David Aaron, Volney Warner, P. X. Kelley, William Quandt, Robert Murray, and Christopher Shoemaker.

12. The definition of this region was a matter of some debate at the time. Ultimately, the region came to include Afghanistan, Bahrain, Djibouti, Eritrea, Ethiopia, Iraq, Iran, Jordan, Kenya,

Kuwait, North Yemen, Oman, Pakistan, Qatar, Saudi Arabia, Somalia, South Yemen, and the United Arab Emirates (UAE). Other terms used are the Middle East, Southwest Asia, or the Indian Ocean region. To avoid confusion, the term Persian Gulf region is used for this broad region, as it was the most common. When the Middle East is used, it denotes the even broader region, including the North African states and the Levant.

13. Indeed, the RDJTF episode could be seen as an important part of the story of the Goldwater-Nichols Act, as it was General David Jones in his role as the Chairman of the Joint Chiefs of Staff who was the first top military official to break ranks on the need for military reorganization. See James R. Locher III, *Victory On The Potomac: The Goldwater-Nichols Act Unifies The Pentagon*, College Station, TX: Texas A&M University Press, 2004, pp. 33ff.

14. National Commission on Terrorist Attacks Upon the United States, "The 9/11 Commission Report," July 22, 2004, available from *www.9-11commission.gov/report/911Report.pdf, p. 353*.

15. Project on National Security Reform, "Forging a New Shield, Executive Summary," November 2008, available from *www.pnsr.org/data/files/pnsr%20forging_exec%20summary_12-2-08. pdf*. It should be noted that this author has contributed a case study to the report, Henrik Bliddal, "The U.S. Intervention in Liberia in 2003," in a jointly edited volume by the Project on National Security Reform and the Strategic Studies Institute, forthcoming 2011.

16. "Forging a New Shield," p. iii.

17. Indeed, Amy B. Zegart's, *Flawed by Design: The Evolution of the CIA, JCS, and NSC*, Stanford, CA: Stanford University Press, 1999; and William T. Schrader's *The Rules of the Game: A New Historical Institutionalist Analysis of U.S. Defense Reorganization*, Ph.D. Thesis, Temple University, 2006, are the only two theoretical studies of how U.S. national security organizations evolve over time. William W. Newmann's, *Managing National Security Policy: The President and the Process*, Pittsburgh, PA: University of Pittsburgh Press, 2003, tackles similar issues, but with a focus on the President's national security processes.

18. Dore Gold, *America, the Gulf, and Israel: Centcom (Central Command) and Emerging US Regional Security Policies in the Mideast*, Jerusalem, Israel, and Boulder, CO: *Jerusalem Post* and Westview Press, 1988. The United States, however, did join the Central Treaty Organization in 1959 as an associate member. If not otherwise noted, this paragraph and the next are based on the same source.

19. Dwight D. Eisenhower, "A Message to Congress, the Eisenhower Doctrine on the Middle East," Paul Halsall, ed., *The Internet Modern History Sourcebook*, January 5, 1957, available from *www.fordham.edu/halsall/mod/1957eisenhowerdoctrine.html*.

20. Steven A. Yetiv, *The Absence of Grand Strategy: The United States in the Persian Gulf, 1972-2005*, Baltimore, MD: Johns Hopkins University Press, 2008, p. 30.

21. In Nixon's own words, "in cases involving other types of aggression, we shall furnish military and economic assistance when requested in accordance with our treaty commitments. But we shall look to the nation directly threatened to assume the primary responsibility of providing the manpower for its defense." See Richard M. Nixon, "Address to the Nation on the War in Vietnam," November 3, 1969, available from *www.presidency.ucsb.edu/ws/index.php?pid=2303*.

22. State Department, Undated Draft Paper, "Instabilities in Southwest Asia—Options for the U.S.," attached to Kreisberg to Ames, Thornton, Murray, Maresca, Memorandum, Southwest Asia Security Paper, JCL, NLC-24-103-5-1-5.

23. Ronald H. Cole, Walter S. Poole, James F. Schnabel, Robert J. Watson, and Willard J. Webb, *The History of the Unified Command Plan, 1946-1999*, Washington, DC: Joint History Office, Office of the Chairman of the Joint Chiefs of Staff, 2003, p. 14-43. If not otherwise noted, this paragraph is based on the same source.

24. Brzezinski to Carter, January 13, 1978, Memorandum, NSC Weekly Report No. 42, JCL, *Zbigniew Brzezinski Collection*, Weekly Reports, Box 41, "Weekly Reports 42-52" folder. If not otherwise noted, this paragraph and the next three are based on the same source.

25. Jimmy Carter, "Inaugural Address of President Jimmy Carter," January 20, 1977, available from *www.jimmycarterlibrary. org/documents/speeches/inaugadd.phtml.*

26. Brzezinski to Carter, February 26, 1977, Memorandum, NSC Weekly Report No. 2, CL, *Zbigniew Brzezinski Collection*, Weekly Reports, Box 41 , "Weekly Reports 1-15" folder. If not otherwise noted, the quotations and references in this paragraph are based on the same source.

27. *Ibid.*

28. Brzezinski to Carter, June 3, 1977, Memorandum, NSC Weekly Report No. 15, JCL, *Zbigniew Brzezinski Collection*, Weekly Reports, Box 41, "Weekly Reports 1-15" folder. If not otherwise noted, the quotations and references in this paragraph are based on the same source.

29. Brzezinski to Carter, June 24, 1977, Memorandum, NSC Weekly Report No. 18, JCL, *Zbigniew Brzezinski Collection*, Weekly Reports, Box 41, "Weekly Reports 16-30" folder. This memorandum contained Hyland's opinion piece, quoted here and in the previous sentence.

30. Brzezinski to Carter, July 8, 1977, Memorandum, NSC Weekly Report No. 20, JCL, *Zbigniew Brzezinski Collection*, Weekly Reports, Box 41, "Weekly Reports 16-30" folder.

31. Brzezinski to Carter, December 9, 1977, Memorandum, NSC Weekly Report No. 39, JCL, *Zbigniew Brzezinski Collection*, Weekly Reports, Box 41, "Weekly Reports 31-41" folder.

32. State Department, "Instabilities in Southwest Asia."

33. CIA, December 1976, Research Study, "The Soviets in the Persian Gulf/Arabian Peninsula — Assets and Prospects," attached to Deputy Director, Office of Regional and Political Analysis, February 10, 1977, Memorandum, Untitled, NLC-25-87-5-1-3. If not otherwise noted, the quotations and references in this paragraph are based on the same source.

34. Carter, "Inaugural Address of President Jimmy Carter."

35. PD-13 demanded unilateral restraint on arms transfers, "Presidential Directive 13, Conventional Arms Transfer Policy," May 13, 1977, available from *www.jimmycarterlibrary.org/documents/pddirectives/pd13.pdf*. For the Conventional Arms Transfer Talks, see, for example, "Summary of Conclusions of Special Coordination Committee Meeting, US-USSR Conventional Arms Transfer," May 24, 1978, JCL, NLC-33-12-3-1-8. For the Indian Ocean Talks, see, for example, the Department of Defense (DoD), Undated, Untitled Paper, JCL, NLC-25-78-1-2-6.

36. State Department, Undated Preparatory Paper, for a meeting with the People's Republic of China, "Middle East Issues," JCL, NLC-4-38-7-2-7.

37. William Odom, January 13, 1981, Paper, "Persian Gulf Security Framework," Library of Congress, Manuscript Division, *William E. Odom Papers*, National Security Affairs Military Assistant, 1977-1981, Box 8, National Security Council, 1980, November-December folder. This is an essay for Brzezinski by Odom that lays out the policy processes surrounding the Persian Gulf Security Framework. It has been used to fill the gaps, whenever the original documents were not yet available and when it provides Odom's own arguments. See also Odom, "The Cold War Origins of the U.S. Central Command," pp. 55f.

38. Brzezinski to Carter, March 25, 1977, Memorandum, NSC Weekly Report No. 6, JCL, *Zbigniew Brzezinski Collection*, Weekly Reports, Box 41, "Weekly Reports 1-15" folder.

39. Presidential Review Memorandum/NSC-10, February 18, 1977, Library of Congress, Manuscript Division, *William E. Odom Papers*, Formerly Classified, 1977-1982, Box 36, "Presidential Directives Regarding Defense Policy Development," Washington, DC: White House, 1977-1982, folder 1 of 2 folders.

40. The Final Report on the Military Force Posture Review has been declassified, and is attached to "Presidential Review Memorandum 10, Comprehensive Net Assessment and Military Force Posture Review," February 18, 1977, available from *www.jimmycarterlibrary.org/documents/prmemorandums/prm10.pdf*. The

documents of the Comparative Net Assessment, however, have not been released yet.

41. NSC, Undated Terms of Reference, PRM/NSC-10, Comprehensive Net Assessment and Military Force Posture Review, attached to Presidential Review Memorandum/NSC-10, February 18, 1977, Library of Congress, Manuscript Division, *William E. Odom Papers*, Formerly Classified, 1977-1982, Box 36, "Presidential Directives Regarding Defense Policy Development," White House, 1977-1982, folder 1 of 2 folders.

42. Summary of Conclusions of Special Coordination Committee Meeting, PRM/NSC-10 Comprehensive Net Assessment, July 7, 1977, JCL, NLC-33-11-3-1-9.

43. *Ibid.*; and Odom, December 24, 1980, Paper, PRM-10/PD-18 Chapter, Library of Congress, Manuscript Division, *William E. Odom Papers*, National Security Affairs Military Assistant, 1977-1981, Box 8, "National Security Council, 1980, November-December" folder. The latter source is an essay for Brzezinski by Odom that lays out the policy processes surrounding PRM-10/PD-18. It has been used to fill the gaps, whenever the original documents were not yet available and when it provides Odom's own arguments.

44. Odom, December 24, 1980, Paper, PRM-10/PD-18.

45. Summary of Conclusions of Special Coordination Committee Meeting, PRM/NSC-10 Comprehensive Net Assessment, July 7, 1977, JCL, NLC-33-11-3-1-9. If not otherwise noted, the quotations and references in this paragraph are based on the same source.

46. Thomson and Utgoff to Brzezinski, July 6, 1977, Memorandum, PRC Meeting on PRM-10—Friday, July 8, 1977, at 10:00 A.M., JCL, *Zbigniew Brzezinski Collection*, Subject File, Box 24, "PRC—22: 7/8/77" folder.

47. Brzezinski to Carter, November 27, 1978, Memorandum, "Information Items," JCL, NLC-2-15-2-1-0.

48. "Presidential Directive 18, US National Strategy," August 26, 1977, available from *www.jimmycarterlibrary.org/documents/pd-directives/pd18.pdf*.

49. Odom, "The Cold War Origins of the U.S. Central Command," p. 59.

50. Odom, December 24, 1980, Paper, PRM-10/PD-18 Chapter. See also Odom, January 13, 1981, Paper, "Persian Gulf Security Framework."

51. Brzezinski to Carter, January 13, 1978, Memorandum, "NSC Weekly Report No. 42."

52. Interview with William Quandt, May 11, 2009.

53. Minutes of Special Coordination Meeting, "The Horn of Africa," February 22, 1978, JCL, *Zbigniew Brzezinski Collection*, Geographic File, Box 11, "Ethiopia-Somalia," 4/77-2/22/78 folder. If not otherwise noted, the quotations and references in this paragraph are based on the same source.

54. "Presidential Directive 32, US Policy toward the Horn of Africa," February 24, 1978, available from *www.jimmycarterlibrary. org/documents/pddirectives/pd32.pdf*.

55. Brzezinski to Carter, June 30, 1978, Memorandum, NSC Weekly Report No. 65, JCL, *Zbigniew Brzezinski Collection*, Weekly Reports, Box 41, "Weekly Reports 61-71" folder. If not otherwise noted, the quotations and references in this paragraph and the next are based on the same source.

56. For example, on July 27, a meeting on Southwest Asia was held, Summary of Conclusions of Policy Review Committee Meeting, South and West Asia, July 27, 1978, JCL, NLC-15-3-5-5-2, which led to a State Department study on regional security. See also Summary of Conclusions of Presidential Review Committee Meeting, PRC on Pakistan—Summary of Conclusions, November 30, 1978, JCL, NLC-25-122-9-14-5.

57. State Department, "Instabilities in Southwest Asia."

58. Brzezinski to Carter, November 3, 1978, Memorandum, NSC Weekly Report No. 78, JCL, *Zbigniew Brzezinski Collection*, Weekly Reports, Box 42, "Weekly Reports 71-81" folder.

59. Sullivan, November 9, 1978, Cable Tehran, "Thinking the Unthinkable," 11039, Digital National Security Archive, Iran Revolution, IR01711.

60. Brzezinski to Carter, December 2, 1978, Memorandum, NSC Weekly Report No. 81, JCL, *Zbigniew Brzezinski Collection*, Weekly Reports, Box 42, "Weekly Reports 71-81" folder. If not otherwise noted, the quotations and references in this paragraph and the next are based on the same source.

61. Minutes of Special Coordination Committee Meeting, "Petroleum Supply Vulnerability Assessment," March 24, 1978, JCL, NLC-31-48-4-9-2.

62. DoD, Undated, Paper, "US Capability to Respond to Limited Contingencies," attached to Brown to Brzezinski, August 16, 1979, Memorandum, "US Capability to Respond to Limited Contingencies," JCL, *Zbigniew Brzezinski Collection*, Geographic File, Box 15, "Southwest Asia-Persian Gulf, 2/79-12/79" folder.

63. Odom, "The Cold War Origins of the U.S. Central Command," p. 58.

64. Njolstad, p. 28.

65. Interview with Robert Murray, May 21, 2009.

66. Odom, January 13, 1981, Paper, "Persian Gulf Security Framework."

67. Interview with Dr. Harold Brown, May 25, 2009.

68. Odom to Brzezinski, January 7, 1980, Memorandum, "Progress on the RDF," attached to Hunter to Odom, January 18, 1980, SCC on Thursday: Action Items, JCL, *Zbigniew Brzezinski Collection*, Subject File, Box 32, "Meetings SCC 254" folder.

69. Odom, "The Cold War Origins of the U.S. Central Command," p. 58.

70. Odom, January 13, 1981, Paper, "Persian Gulf Security Framework." If not otherwise noted, the quotations and references in this paragraph are based on the same source.

71. Interview with Dr. Harold Brown, May 25, 2009.

72. Odom, January 13, 1981, Paper, "Persian Gulf Security Framework."

73. Fritz Ermarth, February 28, 1979, Paper, "Consultative Security Framework for the Middle East," JCL, *Zbigniew Brzezinski Collection*, Geographic File, Box 15, "Southwest Asia-Persian Gulf, 2/79-12/79" folder. If not otherwise noted, the quotations and references in this paragraph are based on the same source.

74. NSC, Undated, "Comprehensive Net Assessment 1978: Overview," attachment to Brzezinski to Carter, March 30, 1979, Memorandum, "NSC Weekly Report No. 92," JCL, *Zbigniew Brzezinski Collection*, Weekly Reports, Box 42, "Weekly Reports 91-101" folder. If not otherwise noted, the quotations and references in this paragraph are based on the same source.

75. Tarnoff to Brzezinski, May 1, 1979, Memorandum, "Comprehensive Net Assessment 1978," CNA-78, JCL, *Zbigniew Brzezinski Collection*, Alpha Channel, Box 20, "Alpha Channel, 5/79-8/79" folder.

76. "Summary of Conclusions of Special Coordination Committee Meeting," *Middle East Security Issues*, May 11, 1979, JCL, NLC-25-97-2-5-1. If not otherwise noted, the quotations and references in this paragraph are based on the same source.

77. Odom, January 13, 1981, Paper, "Persian Gulf Security Framework."

78. Ermarth to Brzezinski, June 20, 1979, Memorandum, "Further Points on Middle East PRCs," JCL, *Zbigniew Brzezinski Collection*, Subject File, Box 25, "Meetings: PRC 112, 6/21/79" folder. If not otherwise noted, the quotations and references in this paragraph are based on the same source.

79. Ermarth and Sick to Brzezinski, June 19, 1979, Memorandum, "PRCs on Middle East/Persian Gulf," JCL, *Zbigniew Brzezinski Collection*, Geographic File, Box 15, "Southwest Asia-Persian Gulf, 2/79-12/79" folder. If not otherwise noted, the quotations and references in this paragraph are based on the same source.

80. JCS, Undated and Untitled Paper, attached to Dalton to Brown, May 10, 1979, Memorandum, "US Strategy and Defense Policy for the Middle East and the Persian Gulf," JCL, NLC-20-24-2-1-0. If not otherwise noted, the quotations and references in this paragraph are based on the same source.

81. DoD, Undated Paper, "Military Presence in the Middle East/Persian Gulf," attached to Dodson to Mondale, Muskie, Brown, Duncan, O'Donovan, Askew, Earle, Jones, and Turner, June 18, 1979, Memorandum, "Agenda and Papers for PRC Meeting," JCL, NLC-20-24-2-1-0. If not otherwise noted, the quotations and references in this paragraph are based on the same source.

82. Odom, January 13, 1981, Paper, "Persian Gulf Security Framework." If not otherwise noted, the quotations and references in this paragraph are based on the same source.

83. Interview with Dr. Christopher Shoemaker, September 3, 2009.

84. Interview with Ambassador David Aaron, June 12, 2009.

85. Interview with Robert Murray, May 21, 2009.

86. Cole *et al.*, p. 56ff. If not otherwise noted, the quotations and references in this paragraph are based on the same source.

87. Interview with Robert Murray, May 21, 2009.

88. Interview with General Volney Warner, May 20 and 27, 2009. If not otherwise noted, the quotations and references in this paragraph and the next are based on the same source.

89. Quoted in Cole *et al.*, p. 31.

90. JCS, prepared by Green, November 6, 1979, Briefing Sheet for the Chairman, JCS, on a Report to Be Considered at the JCS Meeting, November 7, 1979, JCS 2147/627, "Identification of Forces for the Rapid Deployment Joint Task Force," Library of Congress, Manuscript Division, *William E. Odom Papers*, Formerly Classified, 1977-1982, Box 36, "Presidential Directives Regarding Defense Policy Development, Joint Chiefs of Staff Papers, 1980-1981, folder 1 of 3 folders. If not otherwise noted, the quotations and references in this paragraph are based on the same source.

91. Interview with Warner, May 20 and 27, 2009. If not otherwise noted, the quotations and references in this paragraph are based on the same source.

92. Brzezinski to Brown, July 9, 1979, Memorandum, "Persian Gulf Contingency Forces," JCL, *Zbigniew Brzezinski Collection*, Geographic File, Box 15, "Southwest Asia-Persian Gulf, 2/79-12/79" folder.

93. Odom to Brzezinski, July 24, 1979, Memorandum, "Middle East/Persian Gulf Command Structure," Library of Congress, Manuscript Division, *William E. Odom Papers*, Formerly Classified, 1977-1982, Box 36, "Presidential Directives Regarding Defense Policy Development," Washington, DC: White House, 1977-1982, folder 2 of 2 folders. If not otherwise noted, the quotations and references in this paragraph and the next are based on the same source.

94. Underlined in original.

95. This seems not to have been an issue in JCS debates.

96. Odom to Brzezinski, July 24, 1979, Memorandum, "Middle East/Persian Gulf Command Structure." If not otherwise noted, the quotations and references in this paragraph are based on the same source.

97. Odom, January 13, 1981, "Persian Gulf Security Framework."

98. Odom to Brzezinski, July 30, 1979, Memorandum, "Foreign Policy Priorities for the Remainder of the Term," Library of Congress, Washington DC, Manuscript Division, *William E. Odom*

Papers, Formerly Classified, 1977-1982, Box 36, "Presidential Directives Regarding Defense Policy Development," Washington, DC: White House, 1977-1982, folder 2 of 2 folders.

99. Odom, January 13, 1981, "Persian Gulf Security Framework." If not otherwise noted, the quotations and references in this paragraph are based on the same source.

100. DoD, Undated Paper, "US Capability to Respond to Limited Contingencies." If not otherwise noted, the quotations and references in this paragraph are based on the same source.

101. Brzezinski to Carter, Undated Memorandum, "US Capability to Respond to Limited Contingencies," JCL, *Zbigniew Brzezinski Collection*, Geographic File, Box 15, "Southwest Asia-Persian Gulf," 2/79-12/79 folder. If not otherwise noted, the quotations and references in this paragraph are based on the same source.

102. Odom to Brzezinski, November 5, 1979, Memorandum, "Defense Policy: Directions and Priorities," Library of Congress, Washington DC, Manuscript Division, *William E. Odom Papers*, Formerly Classified, 1977-1982, Box 36, "Presidential Directives Regarding Defense Policy Development," Washington, DC: White House, 1977-1982, folder 2 of 2 folders. If not otherwise noted, the quotations and references in this paragraph are based on the same source.

103. Odom to Brzezinski, November 28, 1979, Memorandum, "Strategy for the Persian Gulf in 1980," Library of Congress, Washington DC, Manuscript Division, *William E. Odom Papers*, Formerly Classified, 1977-1982, Box 36, "Presidential Directives regarding Defense Policy Development," White House, 1977-1982, folder 2 of 2 folders.

104. *Ibid.*

105. Interview with Dr. Harold Brown, May 25, 2009. If not otherwise noted, the quotations and references in this paragraph are based on the same source.

106. His emphasis.

107. Interview with Robert Murray, May 21, 2009.

108. Interview with Dr. Christopher Shoemaker, September 3, 2009.

109. Interview with Robert Murray, May 21, 2009.

110. *Ibid.*

111. REDCOM to Lawson and Shutler, Undated Fact Sheet, "Rapid Deployment Joint Task Force," RDJTF, Library of Congress, Manuscript Division, *William E. Odom Papers*, Formerly Classified, 1977-1982, Box 36, "Presidential Directives Regarding Defense Policy Development, Joint Chiefs of Staff Papers, 1980-1981, folder 3 of 3 folders. If not otherwise noted, the quotations and references in this paragraph are based on the same source.

112. JCS, prepared by Green, November 6, 1979, Briefing Sheet for the Chairman, JCS, on a Report to Be Considered at the JCS Meeting, 7 November 1979, JCS 2147/627, "Identification of Forces for the Rapid Deployment Joint Task Force," Library of Congress, Manuscript Division, *William E. Odom Papers*, Formerly Classified, 1977-1982, Box 36, "Presidential Directives Regarding Defense Policy Development," Joint Chiefs of Staff Papers, 1980-1981, folder 1 of 3 folders.

113. Interview with Dr. Harold Brown, May 25, 2009.

114. Interview with Dr. Christopher Shoemaker, September 3, 2009.

115. Vance resigned after the failed rescue mission to free the American hostages in Tehran on April 24, 1980.

116. Interview with Dr. Christopher Shoemaker, September 3, 2009. If not otherwise noted, the quotations and references in this paragraph and the next are based on the same source.

117. Interview with Dr. Harold Brown, May 25, 2009.

118. Brzezinski to Carter, December 26, 1979, Memorandum, "Reflections on Soviet Intervention in Afghanistan," JCL, *Zbigniew Brzezinski Collection*, Geographic File, Box 17, "Southwest Asia-Persian Gulf-Afghanistan," 12/26/79-1/4/80 folder.

119. Brzezinski to Carter, January 9, 1980, Memorandum, "A Long-term Strategy for Coping with the Consequence of the Soviet Action in Afghanistan," JCL, NLC-33-6-2-8-9. If not otherwise noted, the quotations and references in this paragraph are based on the same source.

120. "Presidential Directive 63, "Persian Gulf Security Framework."

121. Brzezinski to Carter, May 16, 1980, Memorandum, NSC Weekly Report No. 141, JCL, *Zbigniew Brzezinski Collection*, Weekly Reports, Box 42, "Weekly Reports 136-150" folder.

122. Odom, January 13, 1981, Paper, "Persian Gulf Security Framework." If not otherwise noted, the quotations and references in this paragraph are based on the same source.

123. For more, see Njolstad; Odom, "The Cold War Origins of the U.S. Central Command"; and Frank L. Jones, "Brzezinski's Forge: Fashioning the Carter Doctrine's Military Instrument," paper prepared for the Gulf and the Globe 2009 Conference at the Center for Middle East and Islamic Studies, U.S. Naval Academy, Annapolis, MD, January 29, 2009.

124 . Aaron to Brzezinski, December 27, 1979, Memorandum, "JCS Briefing on the RDF," attached to Hunter to Odom, January 18, 1980, SCC on Thursday: Action Items, JCL, *Zbigniew Brzezinski Collection*, Subject File, Box 32, "Meetings SCC 254" folder. If not otherwise noted, the quotations and references in this paragraph are based on the same source.

125. Odom to Brzezinski, January 7, 1980, Memorandum, "Progress on the RDF." If not otherwise noted, the quotations and references in this paragraph are based on the same source.

126. Brzezinski to Brown, January 25, 1980, Memorandum, "Strategic Review of our Unified Command Structure," attached to Hunter to Odom, January 18, 1980, SCC on Thursday: Action Items, JCL, *Zbigniew Brzezinski Collection*, Subject File, Box 32, "Meetings SCC 254" folder.

127. Odom, January 13, 1981, Paper, "Persian Gulf Security Framework." If not otherwise noted, the quotations and references in this paragraph are based on the same source.

128. Cole *et al.*, p. 58ff.

129. Aaron to Carter, February 5, 1980, Memorandum, Daily Report, JCL, NLC-1-14-1-10-3.

130. Interview with Warner, May 20 and 27, 2009. If not otherwise noted, the quotations and references in this paragraph and the next are based on the same source.

131. Interview with Robert Murray, May 21, 2009. Emphasis in the original.

132. Interview with Dr. Harold Brown, May 25, 2009.

133. Interview with Warner, May 20 and 27, 2009. If not otherwise noted, the quotations and references in this paragraph are based on the same source.

134. RDJTF, Washington Liaison Office, April 17, 1980, Untitled Paper, Library of Congress, Washington, DC, Manuscript Division, *William E. Odom Papers*, Formerly Classified, 1977-1982, Box 36, "Presidential Directives Regarding Defense Policy Development," Joint Chiefs of Staff Papers, 1980-1981, folder 1 of 3 folders. If not otherwise noted, the quotations and references in this paragraph and the next are based on the same source.

135. Warner via the JCS to Brown, April 21, 1980, Memorandum, "USREDCOM/RDJTF Planning and Command Relationships," Library of Congress, Manuscript Division, *William E. Odom Papers*, Formerly Classified, 1977-1982, Box 36, "Presidential Directives Regarding Defense Policy Development," Joint Chiefs of Staff Papers, 1980-1981, folder 1 of 3 folders. If not otherwise noted, the quotations and references in this paragraph are based on the same source.

136. Interview with Robert Murray, May 21, 2009.

137. Interview with Warner, May 20 and 27, 2009.

138. Warner, July 21, 1980, Cable, "Comments on JCS-proposed Revision of RDJTF TOR [Terms of Reference]," Library of Congress, Manuscript Division, *William E. Odom Papers*, Formerly Classified, 1977-1982, Box 36, "Presidential Directives Regarding Defense Policy Development," Joint Chiefs of Staff Papers, 1980-1981, folder 1 of 3 folders. In the original, the words are all capitalized.

139. Kelley to Warner, June 6, 1980, Memorandum, "Comments on REDCOM Proposed Changes to the RDJTF Terms of Reference," attached to Kelley to Christoph, June 6, 1980, Untitled Handwritten Note, Library of Congress, Manuscript Division, *William E. Odom Papers*, Formerly Classified, 1977-1982, Box 36, "Presidential Directives Regarding Defense Policy Development," Joint Chiefs of Staff Papers, 1980-1981, folder 1 of 3 folders. If not otherwise noted, the quotations and references in this paragraph are based on the same source.

140. Odom to Brzezinski, May 6, 1980, Memorandum, "Persian Gulf Security Framework: Loose Ends," JCL, NLC-12-28-11-12-3. If not otherwise noted, the quotations and references in this paragraph are based on the same source. Interestingly, this is one of the only times that the failed hostage rescue mission (or indeed the hostage crisis, in general) is mentioned in connection with command arrangements. Odom provides a reason for this in 2006: The Holloway Report, which revealed that command arrangements were a major flaw of the operation, "was not completed until several months afterward and thus was not available in time to induce President Carter to direct the creation of a new regional command." Odom, "The Cold War Origins of the U.S. Central Command," p. 74."

141. Odom to Brzezinski, May 12, 1980, Memorandum, "Middle East/Persian Gulf Command Arrangements," Library of Congress, Washington DC, Manuscript Division, *William E. Odom Papers*, Formerly Classified, 1977-1982, Box 36, Presidential Directives Regarding Defense Policy Development, White House, 1977-1982, folder 2 of 2 folders. If not otherwise noted, the quotations and references in this paragraph are based on the same source.

142. Furthermore, the Army's Forces Command, the Air Force's Tactical Air Command and the Navy (as force providers

to the RDJTF) insisted that they would determine the components of the RDJTF. This meant that REDCOM and the RDJTF were "beholden to them for troops and equipment." See also Cole *et al.*, p. 59.

143. Odom to Brzezinski, May 12, 1980, Memorandum, "Middle East/Persian Gulf Command Arrangements."

144. Jones to Brown, July 25, 1980, Memorandum, "Rapid Deployment Joint Task Force: Clarification of Mission and Command Relationship," Library of Congress, Manuscript Division, *William E. Odom Papers*, Formerly Classified, 1977-1982, Box 36, "Presidential Directives Regarding Defense Policy Development," Joint Chiefs of Staff Papers, 1980-1981, folder 1 of 3 folders. If not otherwise noted, the quotations and references in this paragraph are based on the same source.

145. Warner to USREDCOM/JDA and RDJTF, July 30, 1980, Memorandum, "Command and Staff Relationships," Library of Congress, Manuscript Division, *William E. Odom Papers*, Formerly Classified, 1977-1982, Box 36, "Presidential Directives Regarding Defense Policy Development," Joint Chiefs of Staff Papers, 1980-1981, folder 1 of 3 folders.

146. The author is currently working on a paper with a more in-depth account of this crisis. In said paper, the military situation will be central and the heated internal discussions on policy responses secondary.

147. The United States itself is partially responsible for the failure to anticipate the Iranian Revolution. For a view from an NSC staffer in the Carter administration who worked on Iran, see Gary Sick, *All Fall Down: America's Tragic Encounter with Iran*, 1st Ed., New York, NY: Random House, 1985.

148. CIA, Undated Memorandum, "Soviet Union and Southwest Asia," attached to Turner to Carter, Mondale, Vance, Brown and Brzezinski, January 15, 1980, Memorandum, Untitled, JCL, NLC-23-57-12-1-0.

149. CIA, Paper, "Soviet Capabilities and Options for Intervention in Iran," attached to Turner to Carter, Mondale, Vance,

Brown, Brzezinski, and Jones, February 29, 1980, Memorandum, Untitled, NLC-25-43-6-6-5.

150. DoD, Undated Paper, "Military Presence in the Middle East/Persian Gulf, Dodson to Mondale, Muskie, Brown, McIntyre, Jones, and Turner, August 13, 1980, Memorandum, "Agenda for Security Framework SCC-XV," JCL, NLC-17-22-15-2-1.

151. CIA, Undated and Untitled Discussion Paper, attached to Dodson to Mondale, Muskie, Brown, McIntyre, Jones, and Turner, August 21, 1980, Memorandum, "Discussion Papers for Security Framework," JCL, NLC-31-123-6-11-3. If not otherwise noted, the quotations and references in this paragraph are based on the same source.

152. Unknown Sender, August 22, 1980, Memorandum, "USSR/Iran," JCL, NLC-31-11-9-10-5.

153. Interview with Warner, May 20 and 27, 2009.

154. Summary of Conclusions of National Security Council Meeting, "Soviet Military Threat to Iran," September 12, 1980, JCL, *Zbigniew Brzezinski Collection*, Geographic File, Box 16, "Southwest Asia-Persian Gulf," 9/80 folder. If not otherwise noted, the quotations and references in this paragraph are based on the same source.

155. Carter, "State of the Union Address 1980."

156. Summary of Conclusions of Special Coordination Meeting, "Follow-up on Security Framework in the Persian Gulf — XV," August 22, 1980, JCL, *Zbigniew Brzezinski Collection*, Geographic File, Box 16, "Southwest Asia-Persian Gulf," 8/80 folder. If not otherwise noted, the quotations and references in this paragraph are based on the same source.

157. According to Odom, this led to a "marathon review and soul-searching process," as the paper received a level of attention not seen "since the Vietnam War, and probably not even then." Odom to Brzezinski, August 29, 1980, Memorandum, "Soviet [redacted] and the JCS Paper on Strategy Options," JCL, NLC-12-45-8-8-3."

158. *Ibid.*

159. *Ibid.*

160. Unknown Sender, August 22, 1980, Memorandum, "USSR/Iran."

161. *Ibid.*

162. Summary of Conclusions of Special Coordination Meeting, "Follow-up on Security Framework in the Persian Gulf—XVI," September 2, 1980, JCL, *Zbigniew Brzezinski Collection*, Geographic File, Box 16, "Southwest Asia-Persian Gulf," 9/80 folder. If not otherwise noted, the quotations and references in this paragraph and the next are based on the same source.

163. *Ibid.*

164. Summary of Conclusions of National Security Council Meeting, "Soviet Military Threat to Iran," September 12, 1980, JCL, *Zbigniew Brzezinski Collection*, Geographic File, Box 16, "Southwest Asia-Persian Gulf," 9/80 folder.

165. Summary of Conclusions of Special Coordination Meeting, "Follow-up on Security Framework in the Persian Gulf—XVI."

166. State Department, August 21, 1980, Discussion Paper, "Accelerated Diplomatic Strategy," attached to Dodson to Mondale, Muskie, Brown, McIntyre, Jones, and Turner.

167. Undated non-paper for Muskie-Gromyko reference Iran & Persian Gulf area, attached to Muskie to Carter, September 13, 1980, Memorandum, "UN Meeting with Gromyko," JCL, *Zbigniew Brzezinski Collection*, Alpha Channel, Box 20, "Alpha Channel, Miscellaneous," 9/80-10/80 folder.

168. Also, it is not yet clear how the Iraqi invasion of Iran on September 22, 1980, affected this situation. Brzezinski, for one, saw a unique opportunity to consolidate the U.S. security position in the region, as U.S. allies would depend more upon U.S. help.

Brzezinski to Carter, October 3, 1980, Memorandum, "NSC Weekly Report No. 156," JCL, *Zbigniew Brzezinski Collection*, Weekly Reports, Box 42, "Weekly Reports 151-161" folder. In the military's judgment, it did not significantly affect U.S. defense plans for Iran. DoD, November 14, 1980, Draft Paper, "Implications of Iran-Iraq Conflict on US Defense Strategy for the PG/SWA Region," LOC, Manuscript Division, *William E. Odom Papers*, Formerly Classified, 1977-1982, Box 36, "Presidential Directives Regarding Defense Policy Development," Joint Chiefs of Staff Papers, 1980-1981, folder 3 of 3 folders.

169. Interview with Dr. Christopher Shoemaker, September 3, 2009.

170. *Ibid.*

171. Interview with Dr. Harold Brown, May 25, 2009.

172. Odom to Allen, February 11, 1981, Memorandum, "Persian Gulf Security Framework," Library of Congress, Washington, DC, Manuscript Division, *William E. Odom Papers*, Formerly Classified, 1977-1982, Box 36, "Presidential Directives regarding Defense Policy Development," White House, 1977-1982, folder 2 of 2 folders.

173. *Ibid.*

174. *Ibid.*

175. Interview with Dr. Christopher Shoemaker, September 3, 2009. If not otherwise noted, the quotations and references in this paragraph are based on the same source.

176. Cole *et al.*, p. 63ff. If not otherwise noted, the quotations and references in this paragraph are based on the same source.

177. See Zegart; and Schrader.

178. The theoretical argument behind this claim is laid out in the author's M.Sc. thesis. See note 1 for details.

179. Jeffrey W. Taliaferro, Steven E. Lobell, and Norrin M. Ripsman, "Introduction: Neoclassical Realism, the State, and Foreign Policy," in Steven E. Lobell, Norrin M. Ripsman and Jeffrey W. Taliaferro, eds., *Neoclassical Realism, the State, and Foreign Policy*, New York: Cambridge University Press, 2009, p. 25.

180. In the following, the term "bureaucrat" covers all those officials in national security organizations, such as the Department of Defense, below the explicitly political level (for example the Secretary of Defense). It is not used in any pejorative sense, as is sometimes the case in common speech.

181. See, for example, B. Guy Peters, *The Politics of Bureaucracy*, 4th Ed., New York: Longman Publishers, 1995, p. 217; and Philip Selznick, *Leadership in Administration: A Sociological Interpretation*, Evanston, IL: Row, 1957, p. 121.

182. Graham T. Allison and Philip Zelikow, *Essence of Decision: Explaining the Cuban Missile Crisis,* 2nd Ed., New York: Longman, 1999, p. 168.

183. Project on National Security Reform, "Forging a New Shield," pp. i-vi. If not otherwise noted, the quotations and references in this paragraph and the next three are based on the same source.

184. *Ibid.,*p. 83.

185. See, for example, James J. F. Forest and Rebecca Crispin, "AFRICOM: Troubled Infancy, Promising Future," *Contemporary Security Policy*, Vol. 30, No. 1, 2009, p. 6.

186. For a commentary by three former USAID administrators, see J. Brian Atwood, M. Peter McPherson, and Andrew Natsios, "Arrested Development: Making Foreign Aid a More Effective Tool," *Foreign Affairs*, Vol. 87, No. 6, 2008.

ACRONYMS

CENTCOM	Central Command
CIA	Central Intelligence Agency
CINC	Commander in Chief
CINCRED	Commander in Chief, Readiness Command
CJCS	Chairman of the Joint Chiefs of Staff
COMRDJTF	Commander, Rapid Deployment Joint Task Force
DoD	Department of Defense
EUCOM	European Command
JCS	Joint Chiefs of Staff
JTF	Joint Task Force
MIDEASTFOR	Middle East Force
NCA	National Command Authority
NSC	National Security Council
PACOM	Pacific Command
PD	Presidential Directive
PGSF	Persian Gulf Security Framework
PNSR	Project on National Security Reform
PRM	Presidential Review Memorandum
RDF	Rapid Deployment Force
RDJTF	Rapid Deployment Joint Task Force

REDCOM	Readiness Command
SACEUR	Supreme Allied Commander, Europe
STRICOM	Strike Command
UCP	Unified Command Plan
UK	United Kingdom of Great Britain and Northern Ireland
U.S.	United States of America
USSR	Union of Socialist Soviet Republics

www.ingramcontent.com/pod-product-compliance
Lightning Source LLC
Chambersburg PA
CBHW072335290526
45794CB00002B/882